Contents

Handbook for

DISCUSSION
LEADERS

BY

J. JEFFERY AUER
PROFESSOR OF SPEECH, UNIVERSITY OF VIRGINIA

and

HENRY LEE EWBANK
PROFESSOR OF SPEECH, UNIVERSITY OF WISCONSIN

REVISED EDITION

HARPER & BROTHERS, NEW YORK

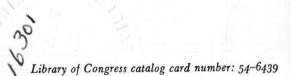

Library of Congress catalog card number: 54–6439

Preface

THIS BOOK IS A COMPLETE REVISION OF ONE WE
first wrote in 1947. But we have not revised our ideas concerning the importance of the discussion method. Indeed, the
past seven years have strengthened our conviction that for
families, informal groups, organizations, and nations, the discussion method is an essential tool for everyday democratic
living. Harry A. Overstreet recently said it this way: "One chief
tragedy in today's world is our widespread inability to communicate. Not only is the Iron Curtain lowered between nations;
it is also daily and hourly lowered between individuals and
groups. Obviously, if in all our practices of life we could learn
to listen and be listened to; if we could grasp what other persons
are saying *as they themselves understand what they are saying,*
the major hostilities of life would disappear, for the simple
reason that misunderstandings would disappear." Skill in discussion, in group and public meetings, is one important ele-
ment in developing mutual understanding and solving common
problems.

We have attempted to provide a step-by-step procedure for
planning, organizing, and leading group and public discussions.
We hope that discussion leaders in schools, service clubs, community forums, church groups, women's clubs, business organizations, labor unions, farm organizations, adult education programs, and other similar groups will find it useful.

To Appleton-Century-Crofts, Inc., publishers of two editions
of our college textbook in discussion and debate, we are indebted
for permission to adapt certain materials. We are also indebted

to the Bureau of Naval Personnel for permission to adapt other materials from a handbook on discussion which we wrote for use in the Navy Educational Services program. And to many others who have practiced, studied, and written about the discussion method, we are also grateful; from them we have learned much that has supplemented our own observation and experience.

J. J. A.
H. L. E.

1.

Understanding the Nature of Discussion

AMERICANS ARE A TALKATIVE PEOPLE, GENERALLY speaking. We like to pick up information and opinions in schools, churches, and at home, by reading books and magazines, listening to our radios, or watching our television screens. Then we like to talk about what we've learned, and occasionally to listen to other people talk. Eventually we make up our minds and cast our votes, sign petitions, speak up in committees, conferences, and public meetings, and tell our friends and neighbors what to think. This is all part of a good American habit that is older than Patrick Henry and as new as the latest Town Meeting of the Air. When the editors of *Time* were summarizing the state of things at mid-century they said it this way: "A significant 20th Century characteristic of U. S. life is the revival of public discussion. There is plenty to talk about. All over the U. S., colleges, newspapers, businessmen's clubs, churches, and women's clubs arrange lectures, forums, panel discussions. Busy and learned men give their time to these gatherings in the American belief that an informed and alert citizenry is the basis of democracy."

All this is true. In the parlor, on street corners, and over the back fence we hold informal discussions about the future of the movie industry, problems of foreign policy, and how to raise our kids. In the P-TA we have committee meetings to decide what playground equipment to buy; at the office we have conferences about advertising policies, or bargaining conferences with union representatives; teachers hold workshops; professional men attend conventions; luncheon clubs hear lectures, panels, or symposiums; and political rallies listen to debates. On all of these occasions we talk. We talk a lot, and sometimes we talk about our ways of talking.

Whenever we try to assess the values of how we talk out our problems, we discover that Americans hold two conflicting attitudes about talk. On the one hand we say that it doesn't make sense to demand "action, not talk," because purposeful talk precedes intelligent action. Some of us may quote the old Greek, Pericles: "We decide or debate carefully, in person, all matters of policy, holding that acts are foredoomed to failure when undertaken undiscussed." Or we may cite English history and recall Macaulay's assertion that "men are never so likely to settle a question rightly as when they discuss it fully." American philosophers agree with Thomas Jefferson that "in a republican nation, whose citizens are to be led by reason and persuasion, and not by force, the art of reasoning becomes of first importance." And Supreme Court Justice Harold H. Burton sums it all up when he says, "I hold to the belief that if folks get around a table and talk things through they usually can come to the right and fair answer." This is one view of the significance of our talking. We believe in the ballot box way of registering decisions, but we also believe in the cracker barrel method of arriving at them. In our clubs, our schools, our businesses, and in our homes, as well as in our government, we hold to the ideal of decision by discussion, majority rule in a climate of free speech.

But we also hold another view about talk when we find it doesn't always live up to our ideal. When Charles Lindbergh made his famous nonstop flight from New York to Paris, Charles F. Kettering heard the news from his wife. "And how wonderful," she concluded, "that he did it all alone!" "It would have been more wonderful," observed the General Motors executive, "if he had done it with a committee!" This is a fair comment on some of our experiences with talk. Committees— and conferences, panels, lectures, and informal discussions, too —are often inefficient. They seem to go nowhere, and take all evening to do it. A writer in the *New Yorker* recently summed up this skeptical point of view:

"All committee meetings, whether of a gambling syndicate or a charity ball, of Communists or State Department officials, have certain qualities in common. Most of the time is taken up with long-winded speeches that either miss the point or labor it to death; the agenda is usually inverted in such a way that the significant items turn up at the end, after hours of trivia; the chairman is either so easygoing that a few glib members monopolize the discussion or so authoritarian that nobody has his say. The average, or untalented, committee member reacts in one of two ways, each of them unfortunate. He simmers with repressed wisdom, antagonizing everyone by his badly concealed impatience and contempt, and, when he finally gets the floor, crams so much into his brief moment that he sounds like a fanatic, if not a madman. Or, more commonly, he becomes so depressed that he cannot express himself at all, and the most ruinous policies are adopted without rousing him from his apathy."

Between these two conflicting American attitudes toward talk there is no place to strike a happy medium. We ought either to find ways of making our discussions approach the ideal concept, or admit we are wrong when we say, in Harold Laski's words, that "the art of public discussion . . . is central to the achievement of the democratic purpose."

As a matter of fact, those who care to look for the evidence will find that across the nation in schools and colleges, in adult education centers, in labor unions, in churches, in businesses and professions, and in all manner of clubs and organizations, there is a vital and fast-growing concern about improving American talk. This concern is not like the "elocution" movement of the last century with its emphasis upon beautiful diction and lessons on the rise and fall of the gesture. It is a different concern from the also growing interest in the useful art of public speaking. It is a concern with good talk, not in the solo performance of the public speaker, but within groups and among people who want to discuss their common problems together, informally and purposefully.

Since this handbook was published in 1947, for example,

articles on discussion and its various uses have appeared in at least 65 business and professional journals. Various educational projects making extensive uses of discussion are currently (1954) in operation. The Junior Town Meeting League (356 Washington St., Middletown, Conn.) is an international organization to foster discussion of current affairs by youth. The Fund for Adult Education, financed by the Ford Foundation, has developed two series of adult education film-discussion programs: "Great Men and Great Issues" and "World Affairs are Your Affairs." (For information address the Film Council of America, 600 Davis St., Evanston, Ill.) The Labor-Management Committee of the National Conference of Christians and Jews (381 Fourth Ave., New York 16, N. Y.) has a discussion project entitled "Team Work in Industry," designed to modify racial and religious prejudices and improve labor-management relations. The Great Books Foundation (Box NN, Chicago 90, Ill.) sponsors discussions on selections from the great books of our Western civilization. The Research Center for Group Dynamics (University of Michigan, Ann Arbor, Mich.) is studying and classifying the behavior of different types of individuals in discussion groups. The National Training Laboratory in Group Development (1201 Sixteenth St., N. W., Washington, D. C.) conducts workshops to train discussion leaders in the theory and practice of group dynamics. Both organizations stress "role playing," especially in dealing with touchy situations. The National Foreman's Institute (100 Garfield Ave., New London, Conn.) advocates the conference method among foremen and with management to share information and avoid conflicts.

I. What We Mean by Discussion

The word "discussion" as commonly used means many things. We say that political candidates discuss campaign issues, the finance committee of the church discusses plans for raising money, a family discusses where to spend its vacation, and we may even "discuss" a raise in pay with the boss. In this book, however, we need a somewhat narrower definition, one which approximates what is meant by those most interested in the current development of discussion. They include political scientists who believe that techniques of discussion are basic to the democratic process, that discussion is an essential tool for government in a period of increasingly complex relationships. Social psychologists, primarily concerned with improved human relations in other areas where people work together—business, religion, and associations of all kinds—consider discussion a basic process. And educators think of it as a basic educational method, especially in adult education, which assumes increasing importance in our age of extended leisure time.

All these groups find it easier to describe discussion than to define it, but they would undoubtedly agree that discussion is a planned, but relatively informal, meeting in which those who attend are invited to join in purposeful talk about a topic or problem of mutual interest, under the guidance of a leader, chairman, or moderator. Each part of this definition is worth singling out for comment.

1. *Planning* in advance is essential to successful discussion; it is futile to rely upon spontaneous combustion to develop profitable talk. The initiative for this planning may be taken by a designated leader, but it is better when at least some members of the group can work on it together.

2. *Informality* is desirable to encourage the fullest possible participation, although the size of the group or audience and the seating arrangements in the meeting place impose some limits. Organized informality best describes this objective.

3. *Participation* is an essential ingredient of good discussion, for this method assumes that each individual may have something of value to contribute, and that the cooperative pooling of all available information is the best way to find the right solution. In small groups everyone who wishes to may speak; in a large public discussion only a few can get the floor, but it should be emphasized that active listening is participation.

4. *Purpose* is essential in good discussion. Merely pleasant or socially useful talk that skips from one topic to another is not discussion as we conceive it.

5. *Leadership*, in some form, is necessary for a successful discussion. In public meetings the leader, chairman, or moderator may be assisted by a recorder and a subject-matter specialist. In small groups whose members know each other, the functions of leadership may be shared by various individuals.

II. Types of Discussion

The general purpose of the meeting, the size of the group, and its progress in analyzing the problem, should determine the form of discussion used in a particular situation. We will describe each type in detail later; here brief definitions will serve our purpose.

A. GROUP DISCUSSION

A *group discussion* includes not more than fifteen or twenty persons, all of whom may take part in the conversation. Members are seated so they may see each other and participate alternately as speakers and listeners. The most common types of group discussion are these:

1. *Informal group discussion.* Not more than twenty people converse, rather than make speeches, about a subject of mutual interest.

2. *Cooperative investigation.* When the group is beginning to analyze a topic about which members have little information, the leader may ask four or five members to read on different subtopics and report their findings as the basis for the discussion.

3. *Committee meeting.* A small group, appointed by the parent organization, meets to investigate a problem and, later, to formulate its report and recommendations.

4. *Conference.* Delegates representing various organizations, sometimes cooperative, sometimes hostile, meet to consider a problem and, if possible, to recommend a joint course of action. At other times the "workshop" or "training conference" may have as its only purpose the acquiring of new knowledge or skills by those taking part.

B. PUBLIC DISCUSSION

A *public discussion* takes place in the presence of an audience. The program consists of conversation or speeches by designated individuals, followed by a *forum period* when audience members question the speakers or enter briefly into the discussion. These are the most common types of public discussion:

1. *Panel forum.* Three or four people with special knowledge

of a topic hold an orderly and logical conversation about it before an audience.

2. *Symposium forum.* Two to four people with special knowledge of a topic make speeches presenting different types of information or different points of view.

3. *Public hearing.* A meeting is called by a committee to investigate a problem, to carry out a government policy, or to give representatives of various groups the chance to present their views on pending legislation.

4. *Lecture forum.* A speech by a person with special qualifications presents information or a point of view on the problem before the group.

5. *Debate forum.* A series of speeches of equal length are delivered by persons with special qualifications for and against a specific proposal or point of view.

6. *Combinations of group and public discussion.* Such meetings as institutes, conventions, and semipublic conferences frequently have a program including small discussions and general sessions. The program for these meetings, often lasting two or three days, may be built around a central theme, and require the services of discussion teams.

Other procedures have been developed by those interested in the discussion method, most of them variations of the types described above, and designed to meet specific situations. Some of these forms will be indicated in later chapters.

The terms *leader, chairman,* and *moderator* are used almost interchangeably by writers on discussion. We speak of *leaders* of informal group discussion, *chairmen* of committees and lecture forums, and *moderators* of public meetings on controversial issues.

III. Purposes of Discussion

For the individual participant, discussion offers training in accurate listening, learning how to give and take criticism, the use of good evidence and straight thinking, as well as when and how to compromise. Participation may also help overcome timidity or stage fright and develop a direct conversational manner of speaking.

As a social process and as a method for cooperative consideration of mutual problems, discussion meetings may have a variety of purposes. These are typical:

1. *To exchange information.* The first step in understanding a problem should be the pooling of available information. An informal luncheon table conversation, a group of people who have just listened to a radio talk, or attended church, may begin such a discussion with "What do you think about . . . ?" School and college classes, study groups of the League of Women Voters, department meetings of the American Association of University Women, and many meetings of such organizations as Rotary and Kiwanis clubs are designed to exchange information. Civic groups sponsor meetings to inform interested citizens about some community problem. Businessmen hold conferences to study new products, review sales records, or consider labor policies. Committee members begin to explore new problems by pooling what they know about them. Essential to the achievement of this purpose is that members have information to share.

2. *To form attitudes.* A major function of many organizations and institutions is to change or create attitudes which will influence, and perhaps determine, individual action when the occasion arises. Churches and schools use discussion for this purpose. So do other groups who sponsor public meetings on topics ranging from America's role in the United Nations to the need for a new schoolhouse. When a judge talks to a service club about juvenile delinquency and answers questions in the forum period, he influences individual attitudes. "Great Books" discussion groups share this purpose. And so may informal talks on such topics as buying life insurance, choosing a career, or revising a school curriculum. These discussions produce attitudes which influence future decisions.

3. *To make decisions.* This is the objective when immediate action is required. Sometimes at this point in problem-solving there is general agreement that one solution is best. If so, it's time to stop discussing and take the necessary action. But discussion of vital questions does not usually result in such unanimity. Consideration of the same evidence often leads honest and intelligent people to widely different conclusions. In such cases the discussion should consider the strengths and weaknesses of

possible solutions. Thus a city council may discuss ways of improving local fire protection, a college faculty may consider areas for curricular expansion, a Rotary committee may evaluate proposals for club service projects, or a family group may consider the merits of mountain or seashore vacations. If different opinions persist, someone should move the adoption of what seems to be the best solution. After each side has presented its arguments, a vote is taken and the will of the majority becomes the official action of the group.

4. *To release tensions.* Sweetness and light do not always prevail among citizens of a community or members of any group. As each faction assures its members of the justice of its views, and attacks the motives of opponents, tensions are likely to increase. A discussion among leaders of the opposing factions is often a first step in breaking such an emotional log jam. If they first consider points on which agreement is likely, and uncover mutual beliefs and interests, they may proceed with less emotion to discuss more controversial issues. A common device used by those who preside over such conferences is to list problems in the order of their difficulty, and then begin the discussion with the least controversial. In this way discussion may release tensions and avoid an ultimate explosion. During the last war management and labor representatives of a midwest industrial firm were summoned to Washington to settle a dispute. By chance both groups flew in the same plane. By the time it arrived they had not only established friendly relations through the discovery of common interests, but had ironed out their troubles and reached an agreement.

5. *To indoctrinate.* It may seem strange to suggest that discussion is sometimes a proper method to "sell" a belief or propagandize for a predetermined course of action. In organizations created for those purposes, however, discussion has a place. Of course the members cannot hold an unprejudiced discussion of questions involving the association's basic beliefs; the membership is unlikely to include doubters and nonbelievers. But members may profitably and properly discuss differences of opinion about ways and means of getting their common beliefs accepted by nonmembers. In sum, discussion in a missionary society is not expected to question the validity of the gospel but to consider

the best ways of spreading it. In such cases the use of discussion to indoctrinate is legitimate.

IV. What Discussion Can Accomplish

In recent years, by testing under experimental conditions as well as by measuring results in everyday practice, we have learned much more about what we can expect from discussion. Some of these findings will be indicated at appropriate places throughout this book; others will be summarized in the final chapter. At this point we wish to cite typical studies which demonstrate the effectiveness of discussion in accomplishing its intended purposes. One series of studies conducted by the Navy illustrates the value of discussion when the purpose is to exchange information. Over half of those taking part in the discussions remembered at least half of the facts presented five weeks earlier. Those who have had experience with classroom lectures and assigned readings as methods of communication should take special note! Other studies have led to similar conclusions: discussion is unusually effective not only for learning new facts, but also for discovering different ways of looking at problems, and for increasing understanding of complex situations.

An extensive field experiment conducted a few years ago by the New York Adult Education Council illustrates the effectiveness of discussion in forming attitudes. Thirty community groups, ranging in size from fourteen to sixty, under skilled leadership, using standard discussion outlines, took up such topics as full employment, housing, and education. While forces other than the discussions were undoubtedly present, nearly one-fourth of those who took part shifted their opinions.

The relationship between exchange of information and the formation of attitudes is also of interest. In some situations it is possible to characterize individual attitudes as "good" or "bad," or desirable and undesirable. This was true in measuring the attitudes of Army men toward the cause for which they were fighting in World War II. By careful research it was discovered that those who gained the most information through discussion were most likely to display the most desirable attitudes. This extensive military research confirmed what has long been found true of civilian discussion groups.

Finally, when the purpose of discussion is to solve problems, to reach decisions, the evidence shows that groups excel individuals. At Columbia University some years ago, a series of small groups was established to discuss certain complicated problems, and the solutions of the groups were compared with those reached by the individuals within them. In dealing with various problems, group solutions were correct from five to seven times as often as the individual solutions. This same conclusion has been reached in subsequent studies, indicating that when the purpose is to make decisions, groups make better ones than do individuals.

V. What Discussion Cannot Accomplish

It is easy when examining such studies to become overly enthusiastic about the discussion method. Similarly, critics may underrate its values. There are occasions when discussion should not be used. Its limitations and misconceptions about it should be clearly understood. Experience has shown these limitations:

1. *Discussion is a slow process.* When immediate action is required even the most democratic organizations delegate to their leaders broad emergency powers. When the schoolhouse is on fire is no time to discuss whether to call the fire department.

2. *Group discussion is inefficient for new problems.* Group members who know little about a topic will succeed only in pooling their ignorance in a discussion. They should prepare themselves with a background of information through reading, attending lectures, or listening to public discussions.

3. *Discussion is a poor method for considering questions of fact.* Discussion is not intended to be a guessing game; when matters of fact are in doubt someone should look them up and report them.

4. *Discussion seldom provides an orderly analysis.* The informality of the process often makes difficult a cohesive statement of all the issues or a sustained presentation of an argument. It may also happen that despite all carefully laid plans, the advocates of one point of view dominate the discussion. Only in symposiums or debates is each point of view guaranteed an equal amount of time.

5. *Discussion sometimes conceals real differences of opinion.*

The notion that conflict should be discouraged may lead discussion groups to conceal or gloss over vital differences of opinion. But avoiding conflict does not resolve it, and the emergence of an apparent majority may be unrealistic in terms of fundamental beliefs.

6. *Discussion does not always encourage adequate preparation.* Invitations to a discussion often stress that "there are to be no speeches. We'll just talk things over informally." Thus participants may not be motivated to prepare adequately. Each counts on others to present information he lacks, to carry on the discussion until he wishes to speak. The result may be impromptu thinking as well as impromptu speaking.

These limitations of discussion should not discourage its use. They only emphasize the necessity for its intelligent use, on the right kinds of topics and problems, after adequate planning, and under optimum conditions of leadership and group behavior. The rest of this book outlines, step by step, the basic procedures which experience and research have shown to be effective in organizing and leading discussions. The reader should understand, however, that studying a book will not train him completely for intelligent leadership and participation. He must learn as well by observing others discuss, and he will master the skills involved only by practicing them.

2.

Understanding the Nature of Group Behavior

THE MOST IMPORTANT THING TO REMEMBER about groups is that they are made up of people. Like your friends, neighbors, and business associates, some are short and squat, some tall and thin. Some are cooperative, some cantankerous. Some think deeply, others quickly, and a few do both. Some crave attention, others avoid it. Some need to be pushed or pulled into group activities, others are self-propelled.

Those who plan discussions cannot know too much about the social, educational, political, and economic status and the affiliations of the individuals constituting their group or audience. But it is not enough to construct a profile such as, "the majority attended college, are in business for themselves, adhere to the Republican party, own their own homes, etc." The organizer of discussions needs also to understand how groups function, how individuals may advance or impede the process of cooperative thinking.

Until recently the behavior of people in groups was generally ignored by writers on discussion. This was not a deliberate silence; instead it resulted from too little knowledge. There is still much to be learned, but we know more about the group process and discussion methods than we did a decade or so ago. Research workers in such fields as speech, social psychology, and education have studied the psychology of groups, group leadership, group membership, and the process by which groups achieve their goals. In this chapter we summarize what is known about these aspects of group behavior.

I. The Concept of the Group

The traditional view of social groups may be summed up in such pat phrases as "birds of a feather flock together," "oil and water don't mix," and "one for all, all for one." Like most slick generalities, these are oversimplified and inaccurate. From those who study the behavior of individuals in groups, we get these three basic ideas.

A. INDIVIDUALS IN GROUPS

1. *Society is built upon group organization.* Individualistic as we are, we seldom act independently; we enter into group relationships, formal or informal, not just for social convenience, but because we are dependent upon groups for our existence. The theory of "survival of the fittest" now applies more to groups than to individuals.

2. *Each individual belongs to overlapping groups.* "Whether we will or no, we are all bundles of hyphens," one observer puts it. We belong to different groups in our capacities of wage earner, citizen, churchgoer, voter, and parent. We contribute, intellectually, emotionally, and financially, to each group, and are in turn influenced by our memberships. Sometimes the several groups to which we belong are compatible, frequently they are in conflict.

3. *Each individual is not only of certain groups but he is also apart from all groups.* The very number of his group affiliations may create pressures that tend to cancel each other out. Then the individual must make intricate adjustments of competing psychological forces in order to reach any decision. As Walter Lippmann observes, "when men strive too fiercely as members of any one group they soon find that they are at war with themselves as members of another group." Thus while we may try to think, believe, and act independently, we do it always in the shadow of the groups to which we belong.

B. SIMILARITIES AMONG GROUPS

Any group, formal or informal, consists of people who at a particular time are organized in a special way for a common purpose. This statement implies correctly that all groups are similar in certain aspects. Among them are these:

1. *Groups are usually built around a common characteristic.* Though members may disagree, even violently, on many things, they agree at least temporarily on the main purpose for which the group organized. This fact tends to develop group cohesiveness and group loyalties.

2. *Groups commonly determine their own membership.* Nonbelievers in the group's cause or program are usually not invited to join. In most cases, they would not care to. This means that groups tend to maintain unity on main objectives, though members may disagree on how to attain it.

3. *Groups tend to be dynamic rather than static.* Even groups devoted to maintaining the *status quo* may be dynamic in developing new methods for resisting change. Other groups are dynamic in that sudden shifts of membership may redefine or replace old objectives. Groups that are literally static seldom survive in our competitive society.

4. *Groups transmit social and cultural values.* This is especially true of family, church, and political groups. Other examples include community theatres, reading circles, art associations, and various types of musical organizations. To the extent that these values are transmitted intentionally, they tend to give stability to a group.

5. *Groups are important in determining "life's chances."* The groups one is "born into" or joins help decide his normal expectations in health, education, wealth, occupation, and basic ideas and values. Group memberships may thus provide a fairly reliable basis for predicting the opportunities that will be open to an individual, what he may become, and what he may think.

C. CHARACTERISTICS OF GROUPS

To the extent that a group is composed of like individuals, it can also be said to have a "group personality." While a personality profile cannot be precisely drawn, these characteristics can be identified in most groups.

1. *Group conformity.* Most of us tend to behave in ways that will gain recognition, admiration, respect, or approval from the groups to which we belong. Through trial and error we have learned that if we conform to accepted standards our group relationships are happier. Thus our beliefs and actions are often influenced more by group opinion than by expert opinion. This is not a rule without exceptions, but it is common enough to be a significant characteristic of group personality. The degree of conformity determines how free members feel to express their own ideas, and how much these ideas are appreciated by others. Some writers call the group atmosphere "permissive" when little conformity is demanded, "autocratic" when initiative is discouraged.

2. *Group prejudices.* Few of us willingly admit holding prejudices which make us intolerant of other people's race, religion, nationality, or social status. But we do know that other people are often prejudiced! In groups of like-minded people prejudice is often clearly evident. In fact the prejudice of an individual may be intensified when he is within his group, and apparent even when he is apart from his fellows.

3. *Group resistance to change.* Social changes within or among groups seldom win complete and immediate acceptance. Thus the degree to which a group resists change, either within the group or in its relations with others, is an important index of the group personality. Equally characteristic may be the group's standard methods for effecting change, whether by dictation of the leader, consensus, or some "middle way."

4. *Group structure.* Research workers have recently studied the status of individuals and their relations to each other, both in the parent organization and through subgroups. These subgroups develop because members have different interests, or because it is more efficient to have various groups working on different association projects, or because it is more convenient to have a number of smaller meetings than one large one. The activities of these subgroups and their relationship to the parent organization may profoundly effect (a) the ways in which members communicate with each other, (b) the ways they feel about

each other, or (c) the ways in which members control each other. In organizations where group procedures have broken down, an analysis of the group structure may be the first step in restoring its usefulness. Some evaluation devices suggested in Chapter 6 are helpful in studying group structure.

5. *Group values.* Any group is likely to endorse and maintain values, or ideals, which differentiate it from others. An analysis of these values will aid in understanding a group's personality. It may also explain the aggressiveness one group displays toward others. And such an analysis of group values will provide a basis for predicting the programs, activities, and actions a group is likely to support.

6. *Group patterns of discussion.* All the characteristics of group personality listed above will influence the method and effectiveness of group discussion. Suppose, for example, that a group has a high regard for majority rule, is accustomed to formal meetings and enforces strict parliamentary rules, makes little resistance to change, encourages members with differing opinions to speak freely, and has few strong prejudices. For such a group, one might be able to predict with considerable accuracy the patterns of discussion most likely to be followed, and to estimate their probable effectiveness.

7. *Group patterns of decision.* In some groups decisions are made by *authority,* the rule of one individual. In more democratic groups decisions are made by *enumeration,* counting votes after adequate discussion. In others, decisions represent a *compromise* between proponents and opponents of a course of action in which members yield part of their views to reach a decision. In a very real sense, a democracy is government by compromise. Under the most favorable conditions, groups may reach decisions by *consensus,* a synthesis of the views of all group members. These favorable conditions seldom exist if a group feels outside pressure, works under a state of tension, or to meet a deadline.

The analysis of any group is not a simple matter. Groups are complex in makeup and intricate in procedures. But if discussion leaders and participants are to function effectively, they must recognize and understand the personality characteristics of their groups.

II. The Concept of Group Leadership

The assertion that "leaders are born, not made," is only partly true. People may become leaders after initial failures and repeated attempts. Moreover, there are degrees of leadership. Some can lead a platoon, others a regiment, while a few can lead an army.

Various researchers have tried to discover whether there are qualities common to all leaders, but the facts are still elusive. One able observer writes, "The precise nature of leadership is one of the most difficult problems in the domain of politics, or, indeed, in social action; yet it is one of the most real phenomena in political or social behavior." We do know that those generally regarded as leaders are likely either to be skilled in human relations, or adept at manipulating and controlling the actions of others. We also know that many acknowledged leaders obtain their status through personal prestige, while others obtain it because they are feared. And we know that some have leadership status because of the formal positions they hold, others are leaders without official sanction. But we seldom find anything that can be called a common "leadership personality." Rather we find that quite different sets of skills and techniques, exercised by different people, bring similar results. And we often discover that a leader who is effective in one situation fails in another.

We conclude, therefore, (a) that leadership is not a stable quality, identifiable in all leaders or in all situations, (b) we need to study leaders in various situations to learn what they do and what the group expects of them. Recent investigations indicate that the following are significant considerations:

1. *The group personality determines its concept of leadership.* As we have indicated, one can estimate the personality of any group in terms of seven basic characteristics. The combination of these characteristics determines whether a group conceives of its leaders as benevolent despots who initiate all action and make all decisions, as mere presiding officers for discussions in which group members decide for themselves, or as something in between.

2. *The group concept of leadership influences the techniques of its leaders.* If members behave as though they want someone to tell them what to do, someone is likely to do just that. Even a leader who encourages members to participate in discussion and make their own decisions may, if they fail to respond promptly, succumb to the temptation to tell them what to do.

3. *The leader's personality and emotional needs determine his concept of leadership.* The personality of a leader may be just as influential in determining the quality of leadership as the personality characteristics of the group. If he likes being a "boss," and demands the emotional satisfactions that autocratic behavior sometimes brings, it will be easy for him to mistrust the intelligence of the group and conclude that he must dominate it. Conversely, if he finds emotional security in "team play," he will not bully but guide and encourage his group to rely upon its own judgment.

4. *The leader's concept of leadership influences his techniques.* The leader who conceives of "boss rule"—benevolent, he is sure—as his proper function, develops appropriate techniques. He sees that a rigid agenda is drawn up for every meeting, leaving nothing to chance; he interposes his own views into the discussion frequently, and uses positive suggestion to see that they are respected. The democratic leader develops other techniques in accord with his philosophy. He encourages the group to develop its own plans, not blocking even spontaneous changes; he keeps his own views in the background, encourages members to participate freely, and helps them to synthesize their views.

We are concerned, in deriving these concepts, with the development of democratic leaders, not autocratic ones. This statement poses many persistent problems concerning group leadership and discussion techniques. Among the questions that frequently plague even the democratic discussion leader are these:

a. How much previous planning and forecasting of the group process is consistent with democratic leadership?

b. How far can the leader let his group "go it alone" without actually frustrating its members?

c. How much should the desire for efficiency in accomplishing group goals influence the leader?

d. How much attention should the leader call to the problem-solving process, when to do so may reduce attention to the problem at hand?

e. How can the leader develop techniques that will utilize his knowledge and ability, yet keep the mood of free group participation?

III. The Concept of Group Membership

A college admissions director once greeted a particular set of recommendations with such joy that his staff came running. "Look," he exclaimed, "here is a boy who is commended by his high school principal as 'a good follower.' We'll admit him without any other evidence. After all, we've already let in four hundred people who've been labeled 'leaders,' and God knows they'll need at least one follower!" This is more than a true and perhaps amusing story. It implies that everyone can be classified as "leader" or "follower," that "once a follower, always a follower," and that followers are second-class citizens. The evidence at hand convinces us that these assumptions are false, that with proper training most of us can become effective leaders, at least of local groups.

Much confusion stems from the tendency to think of "membership" as "followership." One dictionary defines membership as being "an integral part of the whole." Applied to discussion, this means that members should be vitally concerned with the meeting's success and should demonstrate their concern by taking an active part in the group project. This is an ideal rather than the usual situation. You know individuals who just "come along for the ride." We know them too. Some will probably never take an active part in discussion. They may be timid or just not interested. But more are nonparticipants because they do not know what to do. They may have belonged to groups where the leader did not encourage the expression of opposing views. Their training may have been passive acceptance of real or asserted authority.

Training members for active participation is a function of group leadership. Suggestions for doing this appear in later chapters. Here we suggest a number of members' responsibilities. The list includes some designed to give members a sense of having something important to do.

a. Sharing in the development and maintenance of group values and morale.

b. Participating in planning general and specific group goals.

c. Contributing to the group enterprise with assurance that these contributions are desired and will be carefully considered.

d. Undertaking responsibility for a share of the group leadership.

e. Employing appropriate skills and techniques for effective communication within the group.

f. Understanding and adjusting to the emotional needs and tensions of other members.

g. Participating in the evaluation of the group's progress towards its goals and of the techniques it employs.

This list is similar to outlines of the leader's responsibilities. The similarity is intentional. We believe that members of discussion groups should understand and be prepared to share the leadership function. Of course, all members will not be expected to do all these things. Nor is it necessary. We believe, however, that the leader should encourage members to develop leadership skills so they may form and lead other groups.

There has been some talk and writing about "leaderless" discussions. In our opinion, certain leadership functions are essential for purposeful and profitable meetings. But, in small groups, the leader's duties may be shared by various members. We shall speak from time to time of "shared leadership."

IV. The Leadership Function

We use the term "leadership function," rather than "functions of the leader," to emphasize our belief that it is more important that the tasks of leadership be performed than to designate who must do them. The leader, chairman, or moderator, is usually assumed to be responsible for these necessary leadership tasks. But he may share some of these duties with qualified members, and such members may on their own initiative assist in keeping the program on the track and running smoothly. Indeed, one of the obligations of leadership, in the best sense, is to train and encourage members to assume as many of the leadership functions as they can.

Students of discussion sometimes classify members according to their typical participations in meetings. These classifications, sometimes referred to as "member roles," are of two sorts: (a) those pertaining to *group functioning*, i.e., building, improving, and maintaining the group process; (b) those pertaining to *problem solving*, i.e., locating, defining, analyzing, and solving the problem confronting the group. There is no magic in the labels used in the following classifications. They are helpful in identifying and analyzing types of participation in discussion. They may also help members evaluate their own contributions, and those of other members, to the success or failure of the meeting.

A. LEADERSHIP: GROUP FUNCTIONING

These are common types of member roles, contributing to leadership as it affects group functioning:

1. *The morale builder* encourages individual contributors, creates a receptive atmosphere for new points of view, and commends those who deserve it. "That's an important fact to consider, Mary . . ."

2. *The conciliator* recognizes differences of opinion, tries to anticipate conflicts and relieve tensions by stressing common goals and emphasizing cohesiveness. "Are we really as far apart as you seem to think, Jones? After all, we do agree that . . ."

3. *The compromiser* aims at reconciling conflicting views, even if it means modifying his own opinions, and seeks for middle ground in the interests of group harmony. "I'll go halfway with you, Tom, and agree that we . . ."

4. *The expediter* helps the communication process by facilitating the contributions of others, especially when some members may be slowing up that process. "Look, why don't we agree that each person can make a two-minute statement of his views on this point?"

5. *The standard setter* helps maintain a high level of group achievement in the quality of thinking and in solving the problem at hand. "Can we really be satisfied with this analysis? I'm inclined to think we've been pretty hasty . . ."

6. *The process observer,* as the term suggests, does not usually take part in the discussion. He sits on the sidelines and takes notes on the procedure. He may offer suggestions to the leader during the meeting. In the evaluation session afterward he helps members evaluate their own contributions. His duties resemble those of the critic judge of a debate. His function is considered in more detail in Chapter 4.

B. LEADERSHIP: PROBLEM SOLVING

These are common types of member roles, contributing to leadership as it affects problem solving:

1. *The inquirer* is concerned with the raw materials of reasoning; these may be facts or ways of interpreting facts. "Let's get down to cases. Just how many times . . .?"

2. *The contributor* tries to provide the bases for sound discussion by submitting factual information or considered opinions about facts: "I think that the last census actually shows that . . ."

3. *The elaborator* often performs an essential function by translating generalizations into concrete examples, or by projecting the effects of a proposed course of action. "Let's see what would happen if we tried to apply that suggestion to our local situation . . ."

4. *The reviewer* tries to clarify relations among various ideas presented, or attempts to redefine the group position in terms of agreed objectives. "When we began this discussion we thought . . . but now it appears that . . ."

5. *The evaluator* looks at the group's thinking in terms of its own standards. He may raise questions about the evidence and argument, or the practical application of a proposed solution. "It just occurs to me to wonder whether we're going to be satisfied if we decide that . . ."

6. *The energizer* wants to keep the discussion moving, on the beam, and does it by prodding the members, encouraging or arousing them to settle on a course of action. "This discussion is very interesting, but is it really helping to solve our problem?"

7. *The group recorder,* or secretary, summarizes the discussion, noting the most important points and any decisions that may be reached. The recorder's function is presented more fully in Chapter 4.

C. NEGATIVE CONTRIBUTIONS

While we are considering individual contributions to effective group functioning and problem solving, we may as well recognize that in many groups there are members who make only negative contributions to the meeting. Here are a few types:

1. *The dominator* tries to run the show, asserting real or alleged authority, demanding attention, interrupting others, making arbitrary decisions, and insisting upon having the last word. "Now I've had some experience at this sort of thing, and let me tell you what to do . . ."

2. *The blocker* is often a frustrated dominator. When he finds his authority is not conceded, or when the majority is moving in another direction, he becomes stubborn and resists the group on every count. "That idea will never work; you might just as well throw it out . . ."

3. *The cynic* sometimes succeeds the blocker. Thwarted in his isolated position he scoffs at the group process, deliberately provokes conflict, or becomes painfully nonchalant. "It's obvious that you people will never agree; let's call it quits."

4. *The security seeker* may want sympathy, or just personal recognition. In one case he becomes self-deprecatory about his own plight, in the other he continually calls attention to his own apparently unique experiences and accomplishments. "I had worse than that happen to me once . . . and I wish you'd tell me what I should have done."

5. *The lobbyist* is continually plugging his own pet theories, or pleading the special interests of other groups to which he may belong, although he is seldom willing to register as a lobbyist. "Now you understand this makes no difference to me, but don't you think we're being unfair to . . .?"

These labels are simply a convenient way of discussing some specific aspects of group behavior. How to encourage the valuable contributions, and how to decrease the number of negative ones, is the real problem of group leadership. With this problem the rest of our book is concerned.

3.

Planning for Discussion

LOCAL MANUFACTURERS AND STATE INSPECTORS
confer about fire-prevention problems. A class in social studies
meets to discuss responsibilities of citizenship. A board of education committee plans a public discussion about overcrowded
schools. Those who organize such meetings need more than
faith, hope, and charity. They also need careful and hardheaded
planning. Many discussions fail, we believe, not because of what
happens during the meeting, but because of what did *not* happen *before* the meeting. This chapter is devoted to the problems
of planning for successful discussions.

I. Analyzing the Group

The first step in planning any discussion is to learn as much
as possible about those who will take part, as direct participants
or as audience members. Few individuals can make this analysis
as well as a representative committee.

A. GENERAL CHARACTERISTICS

First consider who is sponsoring the meeting. Members of a
Parent-Teachers' Association, for example, come together because of their mutual interests in the schools. Delegates to a
labor-management conference reflect the needs and interests of
those they represent. Even at public meetings, where anyone is
free to attend, audiences usually have mutual interests and purposes. Only those interested in community welfare attend a
meeting to discuss building a new school. A lecture on the
future of the United Nations will attract only those genuinely

concerned with international problems. Beyond this common interest, however, members of public audiences often have different backgrounds and conflicting motivations. As a general rule, the larger the community and the more diversified its population the greater will be these differences. These questions suggest the type of information needed in analyzing the local situation:

a. Are those likely to attend of about the same age level?
b. Will they be drawn from the same neighborhood?
c. Do they include different racial groups?
d. Are they from the same social and economic backgrounds?
e. What are their religious and political affiliations?
f. Have they had similar amounts and kinds of education?
g. What has been their experience with the discussion process?

Not all these factors will be important for every discussion. Racial backgrounds, for example, would be of little consequence in discussing the purchase of new fire-fighting equipment; they might be in considering zoning laws.

B. PAST RESPONSES

The group's reactions to past discussions are useful guides in planning future meetings. Procedures for evaluating discussions are described in Chapter 6. These are some of the questions such evaluations may have answered:

a. How many people attended the meeting?
b. How generally did they participate?
c. What did they seem to get out of the meeting?
d. What evidence was there of postmeeting action?

C. ATTITUDE TOWARD THE PROBLEM

The same group may react quite differently to different problems; those who organize discussions should anticipate the group's reactions to the specific problem to be discussed. The answers to these questions may also suggest that some problems are not appropriate for discussion.

a. What is the relationship of the problem to the specific group? (Is the group's interest only academic, or is it motivated by real wants and needs? Does the group have direct responsibility for decision, or is its conclusion only advisory? How far has the group progressed in thinking about the problem?)

b. What information does the group have on the problem? (And what are its sources of information?)

c. What beliefs or prejudices has the group concerning the problem? (And, if any, from what sources?)

d. What is the attitude of the group toward the problem? (If some solutions have already been advanced, are the members favorable, neutral, or opposed to them?)

e. What time factors are involved? (Must the problem be solved in a single meeting, or can several meetings be held, if necessary?)

II. Choosing the Topic for Discussion

Most committee meetings and conferences are held because a problem exists. A motion establishing a committee states the scope of the inquiry, and often sets the time for the committee to report. A conference of business firms to discuss a joint price policy also has its topic isolated in advance. Some organizations are established to deal with a specific problem, such as the planning council for a Community Chest drive; the only decision necessary is where to begin on the problem. Occasionally informal group discussions may develop spontaneously, as in a high school civics class, the interests of the moment determining the topic. For all other groups, such as those having regular meetings, or sponsoring a series of public discussions, the selection of topics is an important step. Here are three procedures:

A. Program Committee

The most common, and simplest, method of selecting topics is to delegate the task to a program committee. Ordinarily the committee's ideas will come from the purposes of the organization, knowledge of interests of group members, or current affairs. The danger inherent in the program committee method is that members may select questions of interest only to themselves, or those they feel *should* interest others. The best protection against this tendency is to make the committee a fair cross section of the group, in age, sex, occupation, and so on, and to change the membership frequently to bring in new points of view.

B. INTEREST QUESTIONNAIRE

The best method of choosing discussion topics is wide distribution of a carefully designed questionnaire. This may be done by the program committee. The questionnaire lists a number of possible topics to be checked and may request that those who receive it suggest other topics. If the program committee wants other information it may be obtained through the same questionnaire: best time and place for meeting, most popular types of discussion, most desirable length of meeting, names of possible discussion leaders or speakers. More candid reactions are obtained if the questionnaire is returned unsigned, but signed questionnaires have the advantage of providing a checklist of those interested.

A sample questionnaire, designed for a particular group, is included here. Only such parts of it as apply to a local situation should be used, for people usually prefer short forms. If the group is to be organized, questions 1, 2, and 5 will have special value; if it is already operating, questions 3 and 4 are most significant.

DISCUSSION MEETING QUESTIONNAIRE

The Madison Civic Forum is planning a series of public discussions. In order that these meetings may be of greatest interest to you, will you please check your answers to the following questions:

1. Would you like to attend meetings of this sort? __yes; __no.
2. Which of these types of meetings would you prefer? (Check one)
   __a talk, followed by a forum period
   __several talks on different points of view, and a forum
   __a debate, followed by a forum
   __an informal group discussion with a trained leader
3. Which of the following subjects would you personally be most interested in having discussed or in discussing yourself? (check three)

National problems:
___the U. S. and the U. N.
___the Taft-Hartley Act
___public health insurance
___relations with Russia
___control of atomic bombs
___uniform divorce laws
___farm legislation
___public power programs
___conservation
___taxes and the budget
___cost of living
___communism at home

Madison problems:
___new zoning laws
___juvenile delinquency
___traffic safety
___city-manager system
___improving our schools

Personal problems:
___home ownership
___social security
___religion in your life
___use of leisure time
___the teen-agers

4. If there are subjects in which you would be interested, but which are not listed above, please write them in below:

_____

_____

5. What other suggestions do you have that would be helpful in planning discussion meetings that would interest you?

_____

_____

(You may sign your name if you wish)
_____name
_____address
_____home phone

On page 30 is a questionnaire used by an organization with a stable membership and a tradition of monthly meetings. It incorporates tentative suggestions reflecting the program committee's thinking. This gives members something definite to go on, but unless they are highly interested and used to taking part in planning, their responses are likely to endorse the committee's suggestions without question. Even this may be of value as a step in getting the group to undertake some responsibility.

A final word on topic selection: don't avoid local problems on which there are vital differences of opinion. These are topics on which discussion is most needed. The fear that discussion will produce nothing but controversy is without much foundation. Speakers who differ violently are more likely to be courteous and cooperative in face-to-face discussions than in partisan meetings with the opposition absent.

VENABLE SCHOOL P-TA CHECK LIST

It seems desirable to link together the monthly meetings with a sound theme for the year. Your program committee suggests as the 1953–1954 theme: *your responsibility for a better school program.*

Do you approve this theme? ___yes; ___no.

The following suggestions are for your consideration. Please indicate your reaction to each by checking the appropriate blank:

A. Program Suggestions:

1. "What Parents Expect of Teachers and What Teachers Expect of Parents" might be used for one program. The topic would be presented by a panel made up of teachers and parents and be followed by a general discussion period. Do you:
   ___strongly favor this suggestion? ___feel neutral? ___disapprove?

2. It is common practice to use one or more speakers for topics related to the year's theme. Do you think a speaker should be used for:
   ___one program? ___two programs? ___more than two programs?

3. One program might be built around small group discussions of specific topics. Small groups could meet with a discussion leader in classrooms. This would be followed by a general meeting devoted to hearing reports from the smaller groups. Do you:
   ___strongly favor this suggestion? ___feel neutral? ___disapprove?

4. An appropriate educational film followed by general discussion could be used for one program. Do you:
   ___strongly favor this suggestion? ___feel neutral? ___disapprove?

5. One program might be planned around pupil activities. For example: a demonstration type program could be arranged to show what boys and girls are doing in one specific phase of the school program. Do you:
   ___strongly favor this suggestion? ___feel neutral? ___disapprove?

B. A men's night could be planned and scheduled early in the year. This would be primarily a social meeting and would be open to men only. Do you:

___strongly favor this suggestion? ___feel neutral? ___dis-
approve?

C. Do you know a person who could make a contribution in a
program this year?

    1. _____

    2. _____

D. Will you please offer suggestions concerning the program in
general? Are there other program activities you might suggest?

    1. _____

    2. _____

E. Would you like to have a printed or mimeographed copy of
this year's program? ___yes; ___no.

F. Please list below topics you would like to discuss or hear discussed in a meeting this year. For example: parent-teacher
conferences, discipline.

    1. _____

    2. _____

    3. _____

C. Preplanned Discussion Series

Occasionally groups may be formed to discuss an integrated
series of topics, planned around a central theme, and with supplementary films or selected readings. Local groups may obtain
from the sponsors advice on how to establish the series, discussion guides for each topic, kits of reading materials, and in some
cases related films. Such series may be incorporated within the
program plans of women's clubs, farm groups, service clubs, or
labor unions, or sponsored by schools, colleges, community
centers, libraries, or other adult education agencies. The Fund
for Adult Education (address the Film Council of America, 600
Davis St., Evanston, Ill.) has prepared materials for two series
of nine discussions each: "Great Men and Great Issues in Our
American Heritage," and "World Affairs are Your Affairs." The
American Library Association (57 East Huron St., Chicago, Ill.)
sponsors a series built around basic documents in our American
heritage and their application to contemporary problems. The

Great Books Foundation (Box NN, Chicago 90, Ill.) helps local groups organize discussions based on the writings of outstanding thinkers of all times. The American Foundation for Political Education (19 South LaSalle St., Chicago, Ill.) provides readings and discussion suggestions for ten meetings on various problems of public policy.

III. Phrasing the Topic for Discussion

Topics should be phrased in a way that is compelling, attracts attention, and invites discussion. For small groups, committees, or conferences, where the group exists to consider a special topic, and where the general public is not invited, clarity and precision are more important than attracting attention. For public meetings the statement of the topic may help in publicity. Some suggestions follow:

1. *Use question form.* A statement is less likely to attract attention, more likely to seem biased; a question implies a disease needing a cure and starts people thinking. "What should we do to help European recovery?" is better than "The future of Europe." A debate often begins with a resolution: "Resolved, that Centerville should adopt the city-manager form of government." But the question form is usually better: "Should Centerville have a city manager?"

2. *Avoid ambiguity.* A vague or abstract question may be discussed vaguely or abstractly. Questions should be brief and use familiar words, avoiding terms that mean different things to different people. "Conservative" is vague, "statism" is difficult, "pernicious" has emotional overtones, and "inequitable" is ambiguous. "How can we fight the evils of creeping socialism?" has all these limitations. If you mean to discuss public vs. private power projects, try "Should the federal government build and operate power dams on the Missouri River?"

3. *Narrow it down.* Fruitful discussions seldom develop on topics such as "Shall we amend the Constitution?" or "Compulsory military training." The first is a catchall, the second is incomplete; both require too much discussion time for definition and limitation. These are better: "Shall we eliminate the poll tax by constitutional amendment?" and "Should the United

States adopt a one-year compulsory military training program for all able-bodied men over twenty?"

4. *Give it headline value.* Few newspapers carry headlines like this: "The Frequency of Fatalities in Traffic Accidents." They say "Death on the Highway." Headlines attract attention by telling a complete story in short, vivid phrases. Discussion topics should have the same virtues, and for the same reasons.

These questions recently discussed in public meetings are effectively phrased: "What can we do to curb juvenile delinquency in Lorain County?" "Should we support the bond issue to enlarge the city hospital by fifty beds?" "Is your health the nation's business?" "How can we improve the status of the teaching profession in Charlottesville?" and "What effects does a college education have on personal religious beliefs?"

IV. Choosing the Form of Discussion

The tradition of the group may indicate a preferred type of discussion, with well-established patterns for committee meetings and various types of conferences. Public meetings also commonly employ a few basic discussion forms. Those who plan any kind of meeting, however, should choose the specific form of discussion only after considering these factors:

a. The topic
b. How much the members know about the topic
c. The size and personnel of the group or audience
d. The purpose of the meeting
e. The degree of formality desired
f. Whether members can be expected to adopt new procedures

Earlier we proposed brief definitions of four types of group discussion, essentially private meetings and small enough so that all who attend can take part, and six types of public discussion, adapted to general audiences of varying sizes. Now we describe in more detail the (1) informal group discussion, (2) cooperative investigation, (3) committee meeting, (4) conference, (5) panel forum, (6) public hearing, (7) symposium forum, (8) lecture forum, (9) debate forum, and (10) combinations of group and public discussions.

A. INFORMAL GROUP DISCUSSION

The most common characteristics of this type are the limited size of the group, the comparative absence of set speeches, and the assumption that members share equally in the meeting and in responsibility for its outcome. An informal group discussion takes place when not more than fifteen or twenty people talk about a topic of mutual interest under the leadership of a member designated for the occasion. Members come expecting to take an active part; there are no spectators and no one is set apart as an authority.

As its name suggests, such a discussion should be held in surroundings conducive to informality and relaxation. Chairs should be arranged so that each member can see every other member; true conversation seldom develops if people are seated in rows. The spirit of informality is emphasized if everyone, including the leader, remains seated while speaking. Members of the group should refer to each other by name, preferably first names as they become acquainted. There should be no formal speeches; the best discussion results when few "speeches" exceed a minute in length and the total effect is that of expanded conversation. If many more than twenty people attend, some cannot be included in the conversation, and informality is lost. A larger group should be divided into smaller discussions, all coming together later to hear reports from representatives of each group. Or some type of discussion better suited to larger numbers should be used. Profitable discussions may be held, on the other hand, with groups of six or eight interested members.

The primary purpose of many informal group discussions is to share information about a topic. Members should have some information to be shared, so that each learns from the others and compares his opinions with theirs. If the group finds that it has little or no information on the topic, the meeting should be adjourned until this defect can be remedied. A discussion is informal talk, but it should be informed talk.

Other discussions proceed from information sharing to the development of a group consensus. Sometimes this happens in a single meeting, or it may take a series of discussions. On many topics, of course, only individual action can result, such as "Should I buy more life insurance?"

Although the informal group discussion is conducted with a minimum of organization, the leader must start it off and have an outline to guide the conversation, lest it wander aimlessly. Unless the group members are familiar with the discussion method, the success of the meeting depends largely on the leader. His role is treated in a later chapter.

B. COOPERATIVE INVESTIGATION

Suppose, as sometimes happens, an informal discussion group wants to study a topic, or problem, on which the members have little information. Suppose, further, that no one who has made a special study of the topic is available to give the background information in a talk or lecture. In that event, the group may decide to do the work for themselves. Four or five members may volunteer, or be drafted, to conduct a cooperative investigation.

The name describes the procedure. The investigators meet with the leader and make a list of subtopics, or types of information needed for understanding the problem. Each member of the investigating team undertakes to study one of these points and to report his findings. The reports should be informal, but concise. Following the reports, the leader asks other members to add any information they may have, and to question anything they believe inaccurate or unclear. At least half of the meeting should be reserved for informal discussion.

A word of caution is in order. It is easy to give more information than the group can assimilate in a half hour. With apologies to Shakespeare, the discussers are just as sick that surfeit with too much information, as they who starve with nothing.

C. COMMITTEE MEETING

Appointing a committee is a parliamentary procedure for assigning to a few members of an organization a task that cannot efficiently be undertaken by the entire membership. It would be a waste of man power for a hundred people to plan a school picnic, or for our House of Representatives to frame a tax bill in general session. However, interested members may make suggestions to the committee or debate the committee report when it is submitted to the organization for action.

The essential facts about committee procedure are these: (a) the committee is authorized by the parent organization and is responsible to it; (b) the committee's powers and duties are defined in the legislation which creates it, or by the constitution or bylaws of the organization; (c) the committee's powers range from simple investigation of a problem, to recommending a course of action or, occasionally, acting for the organization within fixed limits.

The legislation establishing a committee ordinarily specifies its size; the best number depends upon the nature of the task. Committees of seven, nine, or even more members can work effectively in analyzing a problem and suggesting solutions. A committee of three will be more efficient in such detailed tasks as writing a constitution, drawing up a report, or planning a survey. In any event committees should consist of an odd number of members to facilitate decision making.

Committee meetings should have the atmosphere of informal group discussion and the chairman, the qualifications of a discussion leader. Gathering information and evaluating suggested conclusions should be a cooperative project. Committee procedure should be informal. Voting on specific phases of the problem should be deferred until action is taken on the final report. Presenting this report to the parent organization usually concludes the committee's work.

D. CONFERENCE

The term "conference" has various meanings. We say "Mr. Jones is in conference," when he is talking with a colleague, or attending a meeting of department heads to decide important policy questions. Religious groups hold "conferences" attended by hundreds of delegates. Neither of these represents the type of meetings we are here considering. A conference is a meeting —or series of meetings—of delegates representing different organizations. They meet to consider a mutual problem, and if possible, to agree upon a course of action. Sometimes these delegates have power to act, within prescribed limits, for their organizations. More often they are instructed to present an organizational point of view and to report back the conference findings. In this respect a conference may be similar to a committee; this is also true, except for larger conferences, with respect to the informality of procedures.

Conferences may have different purposes: (a) *to share information without regard to its immediate use,* such as a conference of delegates from churches, schools, and government agencies to discuss the causes of juvenile delinquency, or professional conferences of lawyers, advertising men, or bankers; (b) *to formulate a joint course of action,* such as a conference of delegates from different religious denominations to produce a plan for combined operations in rural areas, or conferences to plan a summer recreation program; (c) *to settle disputes,* such as a labor-management bargaining conference, or political and economic conferences to deal with differences among nations.

The "workshop" or "study conference" may have one or both of the first two objectives. Local government officials may meet on a university campus, for example, to exchange ideas and receive suggestions about administrative procedures. Or a high school faculty may have a preschool conference to make plans for the coming year as well as to compare experiences and study specific problems.

The "training conference" is widely used by business and industry in employee training programs. Its main purpose is to share information, to compare methods of doing a certain job, or in handling a difficult problem. A. M. Cooper (*How to Conduct Conferences,* McGraw-Hill Book Co., 1942) says the conference is "the best method available" for training people in areas in which they have already had practical experience. R. O. Beckman (*How to Train Supervisors,* 4th Rev. Ed., Harper & Brothers, 1952) believes that the failure of many such training programs "suggests the imperative need of intensive attention to problems of discussion technique."

Members of these conferences are usually chosen by foremen, supervisors, or management, and the meetings are generally held on company time. The procedure is that of informal group discussion with the added requirement that the leader must know the problems and speak the language of the group if he is to avoid being called "one of those impractical professors."

The National Conference of Christians and Jews has a conference program called "Teamwork in Industry." Its purpose is to modify prejudices among members of different religions and races, and to improve labor-management relations. The conference is a series of ten weekly meetings of 30 to 35 selected representatives of labor and management. The meetings, 90 minutes in length, are held in the plant on company time. A skilled moderator is assisted by an anthropologist, a psychologist, a specialist in group relations, and clergymen representing Catholic, Jewish, and Protestant faiths. These consultants are present when needed to supply essential information. Each program is evaluated during and after the series by means of interviews, questionnaires, and attitude tests.

Large "open" conferences and institutes which combine group and public meeting procedures are described in the section on public discussions.

Conference membership should be comparatively small; if not, it should be broken into informal subgroups to discuss specific phases of the general topic. Successful conferences most often result when the delegates are about equal in prestige, knowledge of the problem, and ability to express themselves. Because participating groups select their own delegates these factors are often more variable than in other types of discussion.

Conferences often bring together individuals who are not acquainted, and in those called to settle disputes, some who actively dislike each other. Under such circumstances, success or failure largely depends on what happens at the first meeting. How the organizers of a conference can plan for this situation is dealt with in a later chapter, together with the role of the conference chairman.

Whenever possible the conference chairman should be elected by the delegates. When conferences are called by one organization, such as the American Council on Education, that group's president may automatically become chairman, or someone else is chosen in advance by the organizing committee. To avoid charges of prejudice, and to satisfy local pride, especially when conferences deal with intergroup conflicts, it is wise to alternate the chairmanship among leaders of the various delegations. Another procedure, often followed in labor-management conferences, is to have a neutral mediator, or representative of "the public," preside. A conference secretary should write out a summary of what happens at each meeting, based upon shorthand notes or a tape recording, to be read at the beginning of the next session.

E. PANEL FORUM

This type of public discussion derives its name from the fact that a chairman and two to four persons with special knowledge of a topic form a panel, and before an audience which can hear and see them, converse among themselves. Panels may be held before audiences of varying sizes, most of whose members will be listeners only, but some of whom may take part in the forum period. Audience members come because they are interested in the topic or because they want to see what happens when hostile panel members question each other.

Panel members remain seated while speaking, keep their "speeches" brief, call each other by name, and generally behave as they should in any intelligent conversation, except that they must remember to speak loudly enough so that all of the audience may hear. This general spirit of informality characterizes the University of Chicago Round Table and the Northwestern Reviewing Stand broadcasts, giving the listener a feeling of eavesdropping in someone's parlor. As in the informal group, the leader guides the conversation. In the panel, however, the discussion follows an outline previously agreed upon by the participants, and thus moves in a more orderly and logical fashion. When the panel has established a pattern of discussion the leader summarizes briefly and invites audience members to join the conversation. Thus the panel forum begins as a discussion among a selected few and extends to include anyone present who wishes to speak. With audiences not exceeding 200 the spirit of conversation may be maintained. The panel can be used with larger groups, but the speaking inevitably seems more formal, and individual microphones and public address equipment may be needed.

The panel is used to give the audience a better understanding of the problem or to weigh the advantages and disadvantages of proposed solutions or courses of action. Thus listeners need not prepare especially for the meeting, although panel members must. For this reason the panel is usually better for the introduction of a totally new problem than an informal group discussion. Although the panel seldom permits any member an opportunity for unified presentation of his views, it is an excellent device for creating audience interest and a desire for more information about the topic. It also should give the audience the experience of witnessing good-tempered discussion among people with vigorously maintained differences of opinion. The audience may also judge the importance of these differences. Listening to a good panel is an excellent introduction to the discussion method for those who wish to participate in informal group discussions.

F. SYMPOSIUM FORUM

The symposium differs from the panel chiefly in the formality of the opening presentation. The participants are a chairman, or moderator, and from two to four speakers, each of whom talks for a specified time on an assigned phase of the topic. The moderator explains the topic briefly, then introduces the speakers, making clear the part each is to play in the total discussion. At the conclusion the moderator, or someone he selects, may summarize the discussion before inviting audience participation in the forum. Detailed advice on performing these functions is given in a later chapter. America's Town Meeting of the Air, on both radio and television, usually follows the symposium format.

Like the panel, the symposium is used either to give the audience pertinent information about the topic or to consider the relative merits of various solutions to a controversial problem. The number of speakers depends on the number of significant sources of information or points of view that should be considered. However, a program with more than four speakers usually results in inadequate presentation of any proposal.

As contrasted with the panel, the symposium provides more information, and if the speeches are properly related to each other, a more unified consideration of a topic. Participants are more likely to prepare carefully for a definite assignment; they know the spotlight of attention will be on them while they speak. These same considerations make the symposium more formal than the panel and may restrict the conversational character of the forum period. The symposium is essentially a public speaking program; the panel discussion is essentially conversational. For this reason the symposium is better adapted to large audiences.

G. PUBLIC HEARING

Hearings in which citizens and their representatives may speak are designed to maintain communication between people and their governments. We have already described the usual meetings of legislative committees. We refer here to meetings, often arranged by governmental agencies, which citizens are specifically invited to attend. The purpose may be to discover public opinion that can guide agencies in performing their duties. For example, the Federal Communications Commission has broad powers to regulate broadcasting in the public interest. In the process of formulating regulations, it has held public hearings on whether stations should present only one side of a controversial issue, and whether the same individuals should own newspapers, radio, and television stations.

Public hearings are also called by committees appointed to investigate a problem that may or may not require legislative action. Thus the President appoints a Committee on Human Rights or a governor authorizes a committee to investigate the state's educational system.

These meetings are held in an auditorium large enough to accommodate the expected audience. Committee members are usually seated on the platform. In some instances speakers address the audience directly; in others they address the committee, speaking loudly enough so the audience may hear. The committee may require speakers to register in advance and set time limits on each speech. Committee members may question the speaker during his speech, or at its conclusion. This type of meeting has value for local situations, on such topics as schools, traffic problems, and taxation. It is often used by Community Chest committees in hearing requests for funds, and it may be adapted to the needs of other semipublic agencies.

H. LECTURE FORUM

This type of public discussion is most familiar to American audiences. Many luncheon clubs, school classes, and public meetings use it almost exclusively. As someone has said, when three or four Americans get together they form an organization and hire a speaker. The lecture forum consists of a talk or lecture by a speaker who is presumably an authority on his topic, followed by a forum when audience members may ask questions, add to the information presented, or state their opinions. The duties of the chairman or moderator are ordinarily limited to introducing the speaker and taking charge of the forum.

From the standpoint of those who plan public meetings the lecture forum is the simplest to arrange, only one specialist must be obtained, the moderator's duties are light, and it is suited to audiences of any size. The lecture also has audience appeal since it provides an opportunity for an orderly and thorough analysis of a problem, uninterrupted by hostile questions or comments. In this respect even a 30-minute lecture may have an advantage over the panel or symposium. There is also the advantage of familiarity with the method. Finally, most observers agree that the lecture is the most efficient method of presenting new material to an audience. Even when the forum does not contribute substantially to the discussion, it may lead to profitable discussion later.

The lecture also has disadvantages. The lecturer who has studied a problem enough to speak as an expert, particularly on a controversial problem, has usually formed his own opinion as to the solution. It is difficult for him to present other points of view objectively. And if he does not understand the discussion method or the purpose of the meeting he may conclude his speech with an emotional climax that tends to discourage audience participation. Because it is a solo performance some lecturers are overly dogmatic; without equal opportunity for those with contrary views to share the platform the speaker may dominate the meeting. Not all of its disadvantages are inherent; in a later chapter we discuss ways in which they may be overcome or offset.

I. DEBATE FORUM

One of the great traditions in American life is the public debate. As an educational method, a legislative procedure, and a judicial process, it is an essential tool of a democratic society where the majority rules. Debate provides for an orderly and comprehensive review of the arguments for and against a specific proposal before the votes are cast; it also provides a fair method for a minority to challenge an established majority. We pay the salaries of minority members in our state and national legislatures because we want them to oppose in debate majority views on controversial issues.

Essentially a debate is a symposium limited to two points of view, the inevitable consequence when people with fundamentally different beliefs decide what should be done about an important problem. It consists of pro and con speeches of equal length, and a forum period for audience questions and comments. The debate is presided over by a moderator whose special functions we consider later. An interesting variation is the dialogue-debate developed by Theodore Granik on the American Forum of the Air. He secures two speakers who differ, sometimes rather violently, on a "hot" issue, introduces them, asks a question, and in effect, sits back to see what happens. He enters the conversation to ask another question, rap for order if both debaters talk at once, stop a speaker who talks too long, or to clarify a question. There is a brief forum for audience questions. The half-hour program closes with a one-minute summary by each speaker.

While the debate may present much new information, its primary function is to offer an intensive analysis of a particular proposal or of one suggested solution to an audience already well acquainted with the problem. In a Parent-Teacher Association, for example, where the audience knows the school's needs, a debate would be appropriate before a final decision on the question of buying a piano for the auditorium or equipment for the playground. Similarly on the eve of an election a debate between candidates on significant campaign issues may help voters make up their minds. Sometimes debaters favor or oppose a course of action for different reasons. Speakers may also differ in the intensity of their beliefs or they may base their conclusions on different evidence. Because of its competitive nature, the debate forum has a natural audience appeal.

It is evident that debaters approach problems differently than do participants in other types of public discussion. Debaters are advocates; they believe that their study of the problem has led them to the best answer, and they are eager to explain to others how and why they reached their conclusions. Their desire to make converts is quite in order, provided the debaters are not unduly contentious, and that the time has come in public thinking to sum up conflicting views and make a decision. Listening to speeches on both sides of critical issues makes freedom of speech important; this is what happens to those who attend a good debate forum.

J. COMBINATIONS OF GROUP AND PUBLIC DISCUSSIONS

We include here some of the meetings commonly called *institutes, conventions,* and semipublic *conferences.* All of them combine small informal discussions and general sessions, where some type of public discussion is used. The meetings last from one to three days and the programs usually have a central theme or objective. They are sometimes called "work conferences" in contrast to "listening conferences." The "task force" for these meetings includes a general committee that chooses the theme, or objective, and enough discussion teams for the group meetings. Here are typical examples.

The 1953 one-day Institute of the Wisconsin Association for Better Radio and Television is described in some detail to illustrate advance planning and promotion. The printed programs, mailed at least a month in advance, state the institute theme in two ways: "Promote the Kind of Program You Want," and "Let's Team Up for Better Radio and Television." The program includes an imposing list of sponsoring organizations and state agencies: American Association of University Women, American Legion Auxiliary, Congress of Parents and Teachers, Council of Catholic Women, Council of Church Women, Federation of Business and Professional Women, Daughters of Isabella, Federation of Women's Clubs, Home Demonstration Council,

Federation of Music Clubs, University Extension Division, State Department of Public Instruction, State Board of Vocational and Adult Education, State Department of Public Welfare, and the Wisconsin Youth Committee.

Here is the somewhat crowded program schedule, based on an estimated attendance of 200:

9:30– 9:45 A.M. Opening address, "The Program's Purpose and Plan," by the president of the Association.

9:45–10:30 A.M. Demonstration of "Good and Poor Broadcast Drama."

10:35–11:30 A.M. Eight discussion groups on "Radio and Television Drama . . ." [A discussion team, including a leader, a consultant, and a recorder, was provided for each group.]

12:30– 1:00 P.M. Demonstration of TV drama, by two Madison stations.

1:00– 2:15 P.M. Panel forum on "Making Your Opinion Felt," with representatives of eight sponsoring groups, led by George E. Watson, State Superintendent of Public Instruction.

2:15– 2:30 P.M. Report on "The Status of Educational Television," by Milo Swanton, President of Wisconsin's Citizens Committee.

2:30– 3:30 P.M. Address on "Television—?" by Kenneth Bartlett, Vice-President of Syracuse University.

The names and affiliations of the 24 members of the eight discussion teams and the eight panel members appear in the printed program. The panel was too large for effective discussion, but the committee evidently wanted to give that many groups a place on the program. Many of those attending were delegates from sponsoring organizations. The institute's proceedings eventually reached some thousands of Wisconsin citizens.

An example of discussion in a *convention* is the annual meeting of a state farm organization. The executive committee wanted to know what projects should be stressed in the coming year. For the morning session they arranged a 30-minute panel of six members. Each panel member described a project in which he was interested and commented on suggestions by others. The

150 members present were then divided in groups of ten and provided with a list of the proposed projects. The groups were instructed to choose a chairman and secretary, and after a fifteen-minute discussion, to choose the two projects in which they were most interested. They were told that they might vote for projects not proposed by the panel. After the discussion, the group met in general session to hear one-minute reports from the president or secretary of each group. The secretaries filed written reports with the executive committee.

The *work-study conference* attempts to analyze a serious situation confronting those present. Sessions last from a day and a half to three days, depending on the size of the problem. Instead of listening to a program consisting largely of lectures by authorities, each urging his favored solution, delegates spend most of their time in work-study discussion, doing their own thinking and making their own decisions. Of course, they need information. This may come from the delegates, from the local library, or from "resource persons."

The first step in preparing for a work-study conference is the appointment of a conference committee, whose duties begin with the release of advance publicity and terminate with the publication of conference proceedings. The committee is responsible for the selection and training of discussion teams. Each member should have a special assignment. For example, the chairman serves as general coordinator; member *two* is responsible for physical arrangements, audio-visual aids, etc.; member *three* selects and trains discussion leaders; member *four* briefs the group content recorders; and member *five* organizes the group process observers.

Three or four months in advance of the conference, a careful description of its purposes and procedures should be sent to organizations and groups likely to be interested. This should be helpful in selecting delegates. Later a description of the conference and each member's part in it should be sent to each delegate.

A discussion team for each 25 to 30 delegates expected must be selected and trained. The team includes a discussion leader, a content recorder, and a process observer. The *content recorder* prepares after each group meeting a summary of the major issues discussed, agreements reached, any decisions made, and so on. These reports are presented at general sessions so members of each group will know what is happening in the others. The *process observer* studies and records discussion procedures, noting such things as extent of group participation, what the leader does, the "dead spots" in the discussion, group morale, and possible improvements. Members of the discussion teams are usually given a day's instruction, or dress rehearsal, just before the conference convenes. The schedule of a work-study conference would be something like this:

a. A general session explaining and perhaps demonstrating the group discussion procedure and introducing the conference theme or problem.

b. The groups begin to analyze and discuss the problem.

c. A general session in which they report their progress and their problems. They often need more information.

d. The groups continue working for one or two sessions. Between these meetings the discussion teams exchange ideas and receive suggestions from the conference committee.

e. A general session to report progress and get help on new aspects of the problem.

f. The groups prepare their recommendation for presentation to the general session.

g. The last session considers and takes action on resolutions presented by the various groups.

K. VARIATIONS AND COMBINATIONS

There is no magic in method; the goal always is a meeting that serves the needs of the group and fits the occasion. Those who plan group discussions, for example, may find some topics on which "acting it out" first provides the best introduction. This opening presentation of the problem may be in the form of a play. The National Association for Mental Health (1790 Broadway, New York 19, N. Y.) has published several short plays dramatizing some of the more baffling relationships between parents and children, together with a leader's guide for group discussions based upon the problems presented in the plays. Less ambitious, and frequently as provocative, is the device of role playing, the spontaneous enactment by group members of problems or situations. This procedure is described more fully in a later chapter.

Planners of public meetings may also wish to vary the form of discussion. One successful enterprise combines the lecture and panel. It begins with a 30-minute talk by a specialist on the topic, followed by a 20-minute panel among a group of laymen, concluding with a forum period of approximately 30 minutes. Another public discussion series introduces each topic with a documentary film. *Good Speech for Gary,* for example, might be used for a meeting on the place of speech education in the school curriculum, followed by a short talk, or a panel, interpreting the film for local application, and a forum period. A play, role playing, or a dramatized case history are often substituted for an introductory film, and are effective in illuminating problem situations, dramatizing conflicts, or demonstrating techniques. Other devices adapted to public meetings, such as the "buzz session," listening teams, and so on, will be described later. Our final advice here is to encourage group leaders to experiment with these and other variations in an effort to discover the most effective procedures for specific situations.

There is no best type of group or public discussion; each has its special use and value. The choice for a particular meeting should depend on answers to these questions:

a. What is the purpose of the meeting? Is it to arouse interest in a problem, to acquire information about it, to survey all possible solutions, or to make a choice between competing solutions?

b. What is the size of the group?

c. How much information do members have about the topic?

d. How familiar is the group with discussion procedures?

e. What types of discussion is the group used to?

f. How much time is the group willing to devote to a single meeting?

g. Is the group willing to devote more than one meeting to the problem?

h. Are specialists or authorities available to participate in panels, give talks, or serve as consultants?

i. Are skilled discussion leaders, chairmen, or moderators available?

V. Selecting Group Discussion Participants

Those who plan discussion meetings must determine who shall be invited or named to participate. How this is done, who does it, and the qualifications for participants are matters that vary with the type of discussion employed.

A. MEMBERS OF INFORMAL GROUPS

Usually the personnel of the group is established on a membership basis: those who enroll in an adult education class; those who sign up for a particular study group in the League of Women Voters; or those who join the Laymen's League of the church. Here the planning committee and the group leader have little to do with selection; they set up the best program they can for those they know will attend. Other groups have no fixed membership; the planning committee, preferably with the leader, selects discussion topics with a general appeal, announces a time and place, creates interest through advance publicity, and hopes for the best. Under these circumstances plans must be flexible: if 15 or 20 people turn out, the leader follows the normal procedure for an informal group discussion; if the group numbers 40 to 50 the leader must be prepared to divide them into smaller "buzz sessions" or find some other way of accommodating that many.

The organizing committee may extend special invitations to those who can contribute or profit most. Such people would include those with special experiences or backgrounds related to the topic, and those familiar with the discussion method, as well as those who might come primarily to learn from others. Planning committees should also recognize types of persons who are not popular or effective members of discussion groups. Some of them we described in Chapter 2. A. D. Sheffield would add these to the list:

a. The member who is always quoting one source, i.e., her husband, the Constitution, Karl Marx. . . .

b. The person with an emotional fixation on some idea or

panacea which turns him off the main line of thought whenever the pet idea is touched on.

c. The nervously loquacious person who keeps adding to what he (she) has said, seemingly unable to improve on the first statement or to stop.

d. The silent member who sits glumly through the meeting and pronounces judgment to all who will listen after the meeting is over.

e. The watch-in-hand member, and the person who gets up and leaves in the middle of the meeting.

f. The person with a prejudice against discussing a certain subject, using a certain word.

g. The historically minded member who wants to read all the history into the record.

h. The member who constantly urges people to "be simple" in approaching the most complicated problem.

B. COMMITTEE MEMBERS

Committees are either appointed by the presiding officer or elected by the membership. The first method should result in a better-balanced committee; the second may be more democratic. When he appoints the committee, the presiding officer usually designates the chairman. If he does not, the first person named is often regarded as chairman. Where a committee is elected, some organization bylaws provide that the person receiving the largest number of votes becomes chairman. In other groups the committee may be convened by a designated member and the permanent chairman elected. Regardless of the procedure, the chairman should be selected both for his knowledge of the committee's problem and his skill in discussion. Such a person is not necessarily the one who gains his position by the rule of seniority, as in the case of legislative committees. Nor is he always the one who makes the motion which creates the committee.

Earlier in this chapter we spoke of deliberative, executive, and sponsoring committees; in each case different considerations should guide the selection of members. The *deliberative committee*, authorized to investigate a problem and recommend appropriate action, should certainly include representatives of various interests and points of view. Sometimes there should be a combination of men and women, of youth and age, of new members and older ones who know the organization's history and tradition. Often there should be representatives of various political, social, racial, religious, or geographic groups. The committee should be large enough to represent the different groups interested in the topic. This may mean as many as fifteen members, perhaps divided into subcommittees to study different phases of the problem. Qualifications for membership include knowledge of or interest in the problem, willingness to do the work involved, and ability to cooperate with other members. Those who are undesirable members of informal discussion groups are equally out of place on committees. And the stage is set for trouble if committees include individuals who actively dislike each other, or too many who like to tell others what to do.

The committee empowered to act, often called an *executive committee,* should be selected on a different basis. It is established to carry out a plan or project already authorized by the organization. It should be small, usually not more than three persons, chosen from those favoring the project. Members should be selected for their efficiency, dependability, and ability to work together.

The *sponsoring committee* is of quite another sort. Its chief function is to bring favorable attention to an organization or a project by the prestige of its members. Their names are used on letterheads and in publicity releases, and the members sometimes make public appearances in support of the undertaking. Aside from these contributions, members of sponsoring committees may also advise smaller executive committees. Sponsoring committees may be much larger than deliberative or executive committees. They should including well-known representatives of all important groups and interests.

C. Conference Members

Before members or delegates are chosen, the officers of participating organizations should be sure they understand the nature and purpose of the meeting. If the conference is to investigate a problem, knowledge of the subject should be the most important qualification. If the purpose is to agree upon a policy or draw plans for a joint enterprise, delegates should also be familiar with the traditions and practices of the organization they represent. If the conference is for study or training purposes, delegates should have sufficient background to share information and experience and to evaluate that of others. If the conference is called to settle a dispute, delegates should be emotionally stable. In any type of conference the ability to state an argument and maintain a position without calling names or questioning the good faith of others is of the greatest importance. Conferences to settle disputes may otherwise increase hostility instead of lessening it.

In accepting their assignment, delegates should be sure they understand the nature and extent of their authority. When the conference is only to investigate a problem, there is little chance for misunderstanding. The delegates will contribute the information they have and join in the discussion of possible next steps. But the situation is different if the conference is to prepare a formal report or plan of action. Unless the delegates are specifically authorized to act for their association, they will present the conference report at the next organization meeting and move its adoption. In the discussion on the motion they should present the arguments for and against the conference proposal. In this respect their duties resemble those of deliberative committee members.

From a training conference the delegates ordinarily bring no formal report, although they may summarize what they have learned for the benefit of those who did not attend. Delegates to a conference called to settle a controversy are often given authority to make certain concessions in the interests of arriving at a solution acceptable to all parties. If the solution finally adopted goes beyond these limits, the delegates must present it to their associations for ratification or disapproval.

Observation of many conferences indicates that success is most likely when delegates are about equal in prestige, knowledge of the problem, ability to think quickly, and skill in extemporaneous speaking. These qualifications should be accompanied by a willingness to consider opposing arguments and a desire to arrive at a solution acceptable, if not satisfactory, to all.

For conferences large enough to require formal parliamentary procedure in their business meetings, delegates should be familiar with this procedure.

VI. Selecting Public Discussion Participants

The qualities of intellect and personality needed for success in group discussions are equally applicable to those who take part in public meetings. But additional qualifications should also be met by public discussion participants. Their knowledge of the topic should be broader and more specialized. They must have some skill in extemporaneous and in formal speaking. They must display an appreciation of the discussion method, even though their platform prominence might tempt them to become authoritative or dogmatic. And they must be willing to expose their ideas to questions and comments, some unfriendly, in the forum period. From among those who meet these added qualifications, planners of public meetings must select participants who will be acceptable to the audience; this does not mean that they must say only what they think the audience wants to hear, but that their competence and veracity be trusted. Any individual, no matter how informed or skilled, will be a liability if he has had unpleasant personal relations with his listeners.

The purpose of the meeting also controls the selection of those who take part in panels or make talks. If it is to learn about a new topic, speakers must be chosen who can supply appropriate information. If the purpose is to survey the strength and weakness of different solutions to a familiar problem, the participants must hold different conclusions. If the purpose is to analyze different points of view, the speakers should be approximately equal in prominence and skill.

These general considerations governing the choice of public discussion participants should be supplemented by special factors for those taking part in panels and those giving talks.

A. PANEL MEMBERS

Panel participants share the responsibility for planning and conducting their discussion. They should therefore be chosen well in advance, but only after the objective of the meeting has been established. They should not only have special knowledge of the topic, but represent different sources of information or points of view. Otherwise the discussion may be one-sided. It will help in publicity if the names of panel members are well known; when this is not the case a special effort must be made to indicate their qualifications. Conversational ability should be a selection factor, since the audience will expect from a public panel a more cohesive and skillful presentation than often marks the relatively impromptu speaking in an informal discussion. This test of potential panel members should eliminate the dogmatists, the ponderous or plodding thinkers, and those who want to talk all the time.

Panel members should expect to spend some time in special preparation, including attendance at a preliminary planning meeting. This session is an informal discussion out of which an outline is developed for the public meeting. What type of preparation should be expected of the panel member? First, he should analyze the problem to find the vital issues and fit his special knowledge to them. Second, he should have sufficient factual information to support his own contentions. Third, he should prepare to comment intelligently on points made by other panel members. Informed and reasonably skilled conversationalists willing to make this preparation are good members of a panel team.

B. THOSE WHO GIVE TALKS

Ideal speakers for hearings, symposiums, lectures, and debates are hard to find. They should combine prestige, knowledge of the topic, familiarity with the discussion method, and skill in speaking. Unlike panel participants, theirs are solo performances; audiences realize this and expect a higher degree of preparation and quality of performance. "If this fellow," they think, "is going to take up so much time before I have a chance to speak, he'd better have something to say and say it well."

Prestige and knowledge of the problem are important for all speakers in public meetings, since they are usually featured in advance publicity. People ordinarily come to hear only those whom they regard as thoughtful, well-balanced individuals who can speak with some degree of authority. Lack of prestige, however, should not rule out any speaker who has worth-while opinions.

Familiarity with the discussion method, or willingness to learn, is essential. The speaker should realize that discussion is "thought in process" and avoid, until the time for decision, persuasive devices that press for immediate action. This attitude often calls for tentativeness in phrasing: "it seems to me," "on the basis of the information we now have," and so on. The speaker should be willing to think about the problem with other people and fit his talk into the total thought process. In the forum he must display sincere and thoughtful consideration of questions, not an air of "Little man, what now?"

Some skill in speech construction and delivery is a final requisite. Those who attend meetings have a right to expect talks that are interesting, well organized, and expressed in familiar language. They will expect a speaker to provide new information and opinions, but also to recognize that there are distinct limits to how many ideas may be made meaningful in ten or twelve minutes. Listeners in the back rows want to hear what is said; listeners in all rows want a delivery with sufficient variety to avoid dullness and monotony.

VII. Arranging Mechanical Details

We have emphasized the point that those who plan and lead discussion meetings must do more than select a topic and choose participants. Here we offer suggestions for the most commonly encountered physical or mechanical problems.

A. TIME AND PLACE OF MEETING

These factors cannot always be controlled; choices must often be made when no completely satisfactory alternative exists. Group discussions and committee meetings should be held when members are relatively fresh, relaxed, and unhurried, but these conditions seldom prevail at the end of a working day. It is equally undesirable to schedule discussions at an hour when people are counting the minutes until dinner time. If meetings cannot be scheduled at ideal times, one can adjourn them when people become harried and their thinking hurried, and plan to meet again.

Public discussions are planned to attract audiences; this usually means scheduling them in the evenings. About all that can be done is to avoid conflicts with established patterns of the community: know what time people usually eat their evening meal, when regularly scheduled organization meetings are held, and what evenings are most apt to be free from recreational activities, public entertainments, school programs, and athletic contests. Even "I Love Lucy" night on television might be avoided.

Choice of a place for meeting may be equally limited, but we know that if people are genuinely interested discussions can be held in even the most unlikely circumstances. Informal discussions and committee meetings occasion the least difficulty: lounges, offices, parlors, and luncheon tables are all usable, and easy accessibility for all members is the chief concern. Conferences, particularly those dealing with conflict situations, such as some labor-management or student-faculty meetings, are best scheduled on "neutral ground" in order to avoid any setting that may handicap the discussion by seeming favorable to one group. Training conferences which involve use or demonstration of equipment must be held in appropriate circumstances. Conferences for deliberation will be most successful when it is easy for delegates to become well acquainted, in and out of sessions. For this reason many conferences are held in informal and isolated surroundings such as hotel suites, summer campgrounds, "retreats," and school buildings when classes are not in session.

Public discussion meetings should be held in familiar and centrally located spots, equally attractive and convenient for those who might attend. In some communities, such as Des Moines, public school buildings have been used with success; in others a series of Sunday evening meetings has been held in local churches, with a different one playing host each week. Many towns have community centers or municipal auditoriums that are traditional meeting places. When a number of organizations are sponsoring a public meeting it is often prudent to use a public building rather than a place too closely associated with any one sponsor.

B. PHYSICAL SETTING

For informal groups the ideal setting is a pleasant room with reasonably comfortable chairs that can be arranged so that all participants face each other. The Boy Scout campfire circle has much to recommend it; so has the round table. Schoolroom seats, firmly fixed in straight rows, are unsuited to good discussion, and full-sized adults resent child-sized seats. Chairs arranged around tables in the library or the cafeteria will be better. The setting should encourage informality and relaxation; for adult groups this may mean providing coffee and ash trays.

Similar arrangements are desirable for committees and conferences. When much paper work is anticipated, tables are important, and a blackboard that may be seen by all the group is always helpful. Monastic quiet is unnecessary, but an effort should be made, especially in school and office buildings, to hold committee meetings where they will be relatively free from interruption. Many successful committees and conference groups begin with a luncheon or similar occasion for breaking the ice and getting people acquainted before they discuss controversial problems. In arranging meetings those who represent one group or point of view should not sit together. Even seating charts and place cards are proper stratagems to keep the "pros" from sitting across the table from the "cons." For large conferences the use of name tags is almost standard as a means of developing desirable informality.

Larger meeting places are necessary for panels, public hearings, symposiums, lectures, and debates. Usually this means an auditorium, or a room arranged with rows of seats facing the platform. Where groups number less than 100, and a room with movable chairs is available, an effective and less formal plan is to arrange the audience in a half circle. This is particularly true for panels where the forum may become simply an enlarged conversation. A table and chairs, arranged so all members can easily face the audience or turn to each other, are standard panel equipment. Most speakers in a symposium, a lecture, or a debate will appreciate a speaking stand. For public meetings the speakers should be on at least a low platform; few people care to hear but not see those who are talking. In any meeting the audience should be centralized; 100 people scattered in a hall with seats for 500 make a difficult task for any speaker. If seats are stationary, rope off the rear sections; when folding chairs are used, set up a minimum number near the front and set up more later if necessary. Meeting places should be well ventilated and adequately lighted, but lights on the platform should be shielded from the audience.

C. Length of Meeting

Experience is the best guide for determining how long discussions should last. Sometimes, as at noon luncheon meetings of a Kiwanis club, there are definite limits. Another type of limit exists when a committee or conference must report by a fixed deadline. And there are always limits of the flesh; no discussion should be an endurance contest.

For those planning discussions for the first time, or with new groups, these generalizations may help. When small groups discuss informally a subject about which members feel deeply, interest can often be maintained for as long as two hours, but that will be about the limit of steady concentration for most people. A congenial group might discuss a familiar problem with profit in 30 minutes, but informal groups and committees usually proceed slowly. Discussions should be long enough to encourage thoughtful consideration; a good speech may be made on a simple topic in five or ten minutes, but a five- or ten-minute discussion usually gets nowhere. For a public discussion, such as a panel or symposium, where there is to be any considerable audience participation, at least an hour seems necessary; an hour and half is better.

Conference sessions, including work-study conferences, also have limits. One national organization regularly holds three-day conferences. The 30 members meet three hours each morning, three more in the afternoon, not at all in the evening. The executive secretary of this association is probably correct in doubting that members think clearly more than six hours a day.

When should meetings be adjourned? The best time is before the audience has had enough. If a halt is called when interest is still high, informal conversational groups may continue the discussion until the lights are turned out, and people will be more enthusiastic about returning for the next meeting. If it is difficult to guess when the audience has had "enough," the safest rule is to close the meeting when the announced adjournment time has come. Experienced planners set the limits of meetings in advance and publicize them—"Tonight: 8:00 to 9:30"—and see that the moderator remembers them.

Keeping rigidly to the announced adjournment schedule demands that meetings start on time. Few things in public discussions are more irritating than to wait for the curtain to go up, and to listen to the chairman stall in the hope that more people will arrive. Late-comers deserve no special consideration; if they receive none they may arrive promptly next time. Individual speakers in public meetings must also keep to assigned limits. Those who issue invitations should specify the speaker's time limits, and the chairman may add a courteous reminder before the meeting begins, perhaps offering to give a warning signal shortly before the speaker's time is up. For those few speakers who may not respond to these subtleties the chairman needs a firm hand for tugging at coattails, and a strong voice to announce what comes next.

VIII. Planning Audio-Visual Aids

For many eye-minded people seeing is believing, and even the average audience member is likely to get a more vivid realization of a problem from pictures or graphs than from any but highly skilled speakers. Printed or mimeographed discussion outlines make it easier for anyone to listen or participate more intelligently. When discussions are held to learn about a topic it has been found that audio-visual aids may enable participants to acquire as much as 35 per cent more information in a given time, and help them to remember information up to 55 per cent longer than when such aids are not used. These are important conclusions for all who plan group or public discussions.

It cannot be assumed that audio-visual aids will replace other methods of presenting information or points of view; at best they are supplements. A chart or a map is usually designed to serve the same purpose in a discussion as an example in a speech, making abstract materials concrete. A movie or a diagram may give a panoramic view of a problem that would be difficult to condense into words. In every case they must be planned carefully, and used the same way. Among useful audio or visual aids are these:

1. *Outlines,* printed or mimeographed, for group discussions. For informal groups these documents may include pertinent bits of information, statistical tables, and the like, as well as analyses of main and subpoints for discussion. A typed agenda of steps in performing its task may help a committee. For a conference the outline might include a statement of purpose, main topics to be discussed, and a list of delegates and participating organizations. If individual copies of outlines cannot be provided, use a blackboard; if there is no blackboard, use large sheets of butcher paper or newsprint, thumbtacked to the wall.

2. *Programs* for public discussions. Minimum information should be a list of panel members or speakers, brief biographical data about them, and phases of the general topic each will discuss. The chairman or moderator should be named, and the sponsoring organization, or committee, should also be identified. Special instructions concerning audience participation in the forum period are also helpful. As with group discussion outlines, a public discussion program may include a statement about the problem or significant information to help the audience understand it.

3. *Documentary films* can introduce a topic or furnish background information. State departments of education and extension divisions of most state universities publish film catalogues and operate rental services. A *Directory of U. S. Government Films* is published by the Department of Health, Education, and Welfare (Washington 25, D. C.). Most public libraries take the monthly H. W. Wilson Co. *Educational Film Guide, Educational Screen,* or other annotated lists of current films suitable for discussion.

4. *Pictures, cartoons, maps, and posters* may be borrowed from schools and libraries, reproduced in various ways from magazines and newspapers, or created by any imaginative person.

5. *Graphs and charts* must usually be specially prepared for the topic, although they may be patterned after tables or pictograms in textbooks, pamphlets, or periodicals.

6. *Slides and filmstrips* are really special ways of presenting pictures, cartoons, maps, posters, graphs, and charts. Individuals may make up their own, or for some special topics they may be rented or purchased. The latter are listed in the monthly H. W. Wilson Co. *Filmstrip Guide,* and in audio-visual periodicals, usually available in public libraries.

7. *Blackboards* are perhaps the most common media available for presenting charts, diagrams, graphs, maps, pictorial "chalk talks," or lists of items covered by a discussion group. They are particularly helpful for impromptu presentations; in their absence a large sheet of wrapping paper fastened to the wall may serve the same purpose.

8. *Recordings* of significant speeches, discussions, or documentary treatments help provide information or dramatize a topic. Many are available on commercial records; others may be tape-recorded for the occasion. Those available on loan from the Department of Health, Education, and Welfare are listed in the *FREC Radio Script and Transcription Exchange.*

9. *Broadcasts and telecasts* of special events, significant speeches, or current public affairs make timely introductions for group discussions or public meetings.

Each of these types of audio-visual aids requires special handling for effective presentation. Advice on planning a film forum will be given in a later chapter; suggestions for making and using other aids can be found in such books as Edgar Dale's *Audio-Visual Methods in Teaching* (Dryden Press, 1954). Here are a few bits of advice, obvious enough, but sometimes forgotten:

a. Don't make such constant use of audio-visual aids that their value as *aids* wears off.

b. No matter how interesting a film may be, it is only an introduction, not a substitute for discussion.

c. Be sure that maps and pictures are big enough to be seen easily by those in the back rows.

d. Don't have pictures or other aids passed from one group member to another while the discussion goes on. This inevitably distracts the attention of those who pass and those who look.

e. Make charts and graphs big, but keep them simple. Don't crowd in too many details.

f. Don't display the audio-visual aids until it is time to explain them. Otherwise the audience may be wondering what they mean, instead of listening to the discussion.

g. In making charts, use contrasts, by size of figures or objects, by color of chalk, or by variety in type of illustrations, to add emphasis and clarity.

h. Don't talk to the blackboard instead of to the audience. Stand to one side so the audience can see what you are talking about.

i. Experience with television indicates that not more than 30 people can be seated so they can follow a program on the usual receiving set satisfactorily.

Finally we emphasize again the necessity for careful advance planning by those in charge of discussions. Nothing can be more embarrassing to a leader than a last-minute arrangement for a movie projector that won't work, charts and diagrams too small to be seen by the audience, or a supply of outlines and programs without willing hands to distribute them.

IX. Publicizing the Meeting

To what avail is a well-planned discussion if nobody comes? Good planning includes publicizing. This is true for group discussions as well as for public ones. Seldom do all members of any organization attend all meetings. Aside from obviously unavoidable absences, this is a problem that challenges those who plan discussions. An attack upon it involves sound answers to these questions:

a. Is the topic a vital one which really concerns the group members, or those who might attend public meetings?

b. Have conflicts with competing activities been avoided so far as possible?

c. Are the essential facts about the topic and the way it will be discussed sufficiently advertised?

d. Do people have a clear idea about time and place of meeting?

e. Has there been a deliberate attempt to publicize the meeting?

A good discussion program, once established, will go a long way on its own momentum; launching a new program is a more difficult task. In either case the suggestions which follow will help in planning publicity.

1. *Personal contacts.* Informal groups and organizations with limited membership commonly rely on individual reminders of meetings: postcard announcements from the secretary, phone calls, or an advance calendar distributed at the first meeting. The program committee, if it is a good cross section, may also be valuable in urging representative people to attend, and in issuing special invitations to those who should be interested in the topic or who could make special contributions to the discussion.

A program committee may serve the same function for public meetings. One reason for using large sponsoring committees is to appeal to wider audiences; a large and representative committee of sponsors also avoids the possibility of seeming to ignore some interested groups. Many organizations use a telephone committee to issue individual and personal invitations. One frequent complaint about some public discussions is that most of those who attend hold the same views; thus they become protest meetings or propaganda affairs. The best precaution against this is a special effort to have those present who hold differing views.

2. *Newspaper publicity.* In addition to paid advertisements discussion meetings may be announced in legitimate news stories. These should focus on traditional interest-creating items: the timeliness, significance, or controversial nature of the topic; names and reputations of those who will speak; and names and affiliations of members of the sponsoring committee. In addition to publicizing the meeting, these news stories also provide reminders for group members. Many papers run daily calendars of coming events, and welcome brief announcements.

3. *Radio and television publicity.* Many local radio and television stations schedule "bulletin board" periods for free announcements of organizations or public meetings. Local newscasts may also cover meetings, and it is often possible to arrange for interviews, panels, or short talks calling attention to the meeting, the topic, those who will speak, and the sponsoring groups.

4. *Posters and handbills.* Most communities have traditional

bulletin boards for posting general announcements. These may be in store windows, school buildings, and libraries. Lively and colorful posters should include the essential information about time and place of meeting, topic, and participants. Posters may also include information about the topic through photographs, newspaper clippings, maps, graphs, charts, pictograms, or capsule statements of fact and opinion. While professional assistance in preparing these displays will help, homemade ones can attract attention and create interest if they are simple, colorful, and direct. Many of these same ideas can be used in designing handbills for door-to-door distribution.

5. *Library displays.* The techniques just described may be effectively supplemented by arranging with local and school libraries to display books, pamphlets, or periodical articles related to the topic. Many libraries have special showplaces for such displays. Sometimes a question box may be added, with slips of paper on which people may write questions they would like discussed at the meeting, or suggestions for future topics.

6. *Other announcements.* Occasionally a movie shown at local theaters, or in school assemblies, provides an opportunity for a tie-in with a discussion meeting. These may be feature films, documentaries, short subjects, or newsreels. Perhaps a slide announcement of the discussion can be flashed on the screen before or after the film, or the signficance of the film for the discussion may be noted in news stories. Oral announcements, made at club meetings, in churches or schools, also reach those who may be interested.

Additional suggestions for those who plan and publicize club meetings, informal discussions, and public meetings may be obtained from many special sources. Some magazines, like *McCall's* (Dayton 1, Ohio), *Reader's Digest* (Pleasantville, N. Y.), and *Time* (9 Rockefeller Plaza, New York 20, N. Y.), offer regular weekly or monthly club program suggestions and discussion guides. Organizations like the Community Relations Service (386 Fourth Ave., New York 16, N. Y.), Cooperative League of America (343 South Dearborn St., Chicago 4, Ill.), and the League of Women Voters (726 Jackson Pl., Washington 6, D. C.) distribute materials on planning, promoting, and leading discussions. Agencies such as the Great Books Foundation and the Fund for Adult Education include in their kits of materials for discussion series, described earlier, manuals on how to organize groups, select leaders, set up meetings, finance the series, and publicize the programs. And some organization journals, such as the *National Parent-Teacher*, include program suggestions, resource materials, and discussion guides in each issue.

In any effort to publicize discussions two points should be remembered: (a) stress the fact that everyone attending the meeting will have an opportunity to take part, either as a group participant, or by speaking in the forum period; (b) stress the significance of the topic for the known wants, interests, and attitudes of the potential audience. People are most likely to attend discussions they feel will closely and personally affect them.

4.

The Leader of Group Discussion

WRITERS ON DISCUSSION DIFFER ON SOME POINTS, but not on the importance of the leader. They agree that the success of a discussion depends largely on the leader's skill in getting people to think and work together. Exceptions occur in informal group discussions and committee meetings when the members are familiar with discussion methods and can share in the leadership function. When we list the qualifications and skills regarded by various writers as essential for success in leading discussion, we can readily understand why a group member would want to refuse such an assignment.

Relatively few persons have the combination of personality, knowledge, and skill needed to serve as moderator for a network radio discussion or to preside over a conference between representatives of labor and management. But there are relatively few such occasions, while there are thousands of community groups needing discussion leaders. In every group there are members with some leadership experience who can preside at the first meetings, learning from experience, and from observing the work of others. We would think it unreasonable for a high school lad to refuse to play quarterback because he felt he would not be good enough to play in the Rose Bowl. If, however, he does not have the qualifications of a good high school quarterback, he would do well to try for some other position on the team. The analogy, though not perfect, is, we think,

66

pertinent. Some members of the football squad are better qualified than the others to be quarterback. Some members of the group are better qualified than others to lead discussions.

The Fund for Adult Education reports that one of its objectives in the film-discussion series, "Great Men and Great Issues," was to see "if a combination of biographical films, especially prepared essays, and discussion leaders' guides could aid groups with relatively untrained leaders to fruitful discussion of important issues." More than half of the groups in the test run of these programs had inexperienced leaders. Ninety per cent of these reported a successful experience.

I. General Qualifications of the Leader

To aid in choosing members best qualified to lead different types of discussions, we raise these questions: (a) What kind of person should he be? (b) What should he know about discussion?

A. THE LEADER'S PERSONALITY

The following abilities and qualities should be considered in choosing discussion leaders:

1. *Ability to think and act quickly.* The unexpected is always happening in discussion meetings, and the leader may need to change his plans on the spur of the moment. If he is easily upset by this necessity, he may do well at presiding over a commencement exercise but he is not equipped to handle the rapid give and take of a discussion. Like the umpire of a baseball game, he must be able to make quick decisions.

2. *Ability to get along with others.* The discussion leader's task is to get group members to think "out loud" together. The conference chairman often has the added problem of composing differences and dealing with personality clashes among delegates. These tasks are difficult enough when the leader is well liked and emotionally stable. If he is inclined to "fly off the handle," he should not attempt to lead discussions on hot issues.

3. *Respect for the opinions of others.* The leader must be a good listener genuinely interested in what others know and believe. Those who believe people should be told what to think

and do are irritating enough as group members or forum speakers. Certainly they should not be leaders. Nor should the leader show impatience if the meeting moves slowly or the members prefer their own plan to his. If he shows he doesn't like what they are doing, they will make it unanimous by not liking him.

4. *Willingness to remain in the background*. The leader who cannot resist the temptation to parade his own knowledge, or to point out the mistakes of others, is about as popular as the football star who wants to carry the ball when there is a good chance for a touchdown. This does not mean the leader should let others take control of the meeting. He keeps attention focused on what others know and think about the topic. Instead of voicing opinions, he asks questions. Whenever possible he has the group decide matters of procedure, but he guides the progress of the meeting none the less.

5. *Freedom from prejudice*. It would be impossible to find a leader absolutely free from prejudice on the controversial issues considered in discussion meetings. The practical question is whether the individual recognizes his own prejudice, and whether it makes him unacceptable to the group. Individuals should not lead public discussions on topics touching their personal or professional interests. A football coach is prejudiced on the values of football; a professor, on faculty salaries; a labor leader, on strikes. An individual who has published his views on a controversial issue should not lead public discussions on it. Such persons may lead discussions on these topics within their own groups, but in public meetings they should appear as sources of information or advocates of their points of view.

B. The Leader's Knowledge and Skills

The prospective leader's knowledge of the discussion process, his ability to analyze evidence and reasoning, his skill in speaking and in asking questions, are important qualifications.

1. *Knowledge of the discussion method*. This is the most important qualification of the successful leader. He must know both the why and the how, the purpose and the procedure agreed upon for the meeting he is to lead.

THE LEADER OF GROUP DISCUSSION

2. *Knowledge of evidence and reasoning.* The fact that discussion is as informal as conversation does not justify assertions without proof, or conclusions not based on evidence. The leader should have a working knowledge of evidence and arguments.

3. *Knowledge of the topic.* The leader should have a general knowledge of the topic, but he should represent the laymen who raises questions, not the authority who answers them. Men like George V. Denny, Jr., who served as moderator of America's Town Meeting of the Air for years, could not possibly master a new topic each week. Such men should learn as much as they can about the topic, but their main task is to help the audience analyze it.

4. *Skill in asking questions.* The leader should be neutral about decisions made by the group, but he should be constantly concerned about the quality of the evidence and reasoning. He can best guard against hasty decisions based on poor evidence and faulty reasoning by asking questions instead of voicing his opinion. Questions such as those in the following list may also be useful in keeping attention focused on the discussion rather than on the leader, and in handling typical situations that arise with some frequency during discussion meetings.

a. *To call attention to a point that has not been considered:* "Has anyone thought about this phase of the problem?"

b. *To question the strength of an argument:* "What reasons do we have for accepting this argument?"

c. *To get back to causes:* "Why do you suppose Doakes takes this position?"

d. *To question the source of information or argument:* "Who gathered these statistics that you spoke of?" "Who is Mr. Gish whose opinion has been quoted?" "Do you know that as a fact, or is it your opinion?"

e. *To suggest that the discussion is wandering from the point:* "Can someone tell me what bearing this has on our problem?" "Your point is an interesting one, but can't we get back to our subject?"

f. *To suggest that no new information is being added:* "Can anyone add anything to the information already given on this point?"

g. *To call attention to the difficulty or complexity of the problem:* "Aren't we beginning to understand why our legislators haven't solved this problem?"

h. *To register steps of agreement (or disagreement):* "Am I correct in assuming that we all agree (or disagree) on this point?"

i. *To bring the generalizing speaker down to earth:* "Can you give us a specific example on that point?" "Your general idea is good, but I wonder if we can't make it more concrete. Does anyone know of a case . . .?"

j. *To handle the impatient, cure-all member:* "But would your plan work in all cases? Who has an idea on that?" "Hadn't we better reserve judgment until we all know more about this problem?"

k. *To suggest that personalities be avoided:* "I wonder what bearing this has on the question before us?"

l. *To suggest that some are talking too much:* "Are there those who haven't spoken who have ideas they would like to present?"

m. *To suggest the value of compromise:* "Do you suppose the best course of action lies somewhere between these two points of view?"

n. *To suggest that the group may be prejudiced:* "Is our personal interest in this question causing us to overlook the interests of other groups?"

o. *To draw the timid but informed member into the discussion:* "Spelvin, here, lived for quite a while in China. Suppose we ask him whether he ever saw . . .?"

p. *To handle a question the leader can't answer:* "I don't know. Who does?"

q. *To encourage a speaker to talk with the group, not at the leader:* "Don't you think you'll be heard better if you face the rest of the group?"

r. *To cut off a speaker who is too long-winded:* "While we're on this point, let's hear from some of the others. Can we save your other point until later?"

s. *To take the play away from a verbose member:* "You've raised a number of interesting points which should keep us busy a good while. Would anyone else like to comment on them?"

t. *To help the member who has difficulty expressing himself:* "I wonder if what you're saying isn't this . . .?" "Doesn't what you've said tie in with our subject something like this . . .?"

u. *To encourage further questions by friendly comment:* "That's a good question. I'm glad you raised it. Anyone have an answer?"

v. *To break up a heated argument:* "I think we all know how Jones and Smith feel about this. Now who else would like to get in on it?"

In using questions to call attention to weaknesses in evidence or procedure the leader must be careful to avoid statements that might indicate his own opinions on the question under discussion. Even such comments as "I'm sure we all agree with John's excellent analysis of the problem" should be avoided.

5. *Skill in speaking.* A prospective discussion leader should not decline to serve because he is not an accomplished public speaker. But he should have some skill in clear and direct conversation. This means, among other things, short sentences, simple words, and the personal pronouns we use in talking with others. The leader should ask himself, "How can I make what I want to say clear to these people?" This need not rule out technical terms, but it does mean that such terms should be explained in familiar words. Those who wish to learn more about making meanings clear should read *The Art of Readable Writing* by Rudolf Flesch (Harper & Brothers, 1949).

II. The Role of the Leader in Group Discussion

The leader's job in most group discussion can be described under two headings: advance preparations and conducting the meeting. Since the cooperative investigation is closely allied to informal group discussion, it will not be treated separately.

A. PREPARING FOR GROUP DISCUSSION

1. *Analyzing the group.* The leader's first step should be to find out as much as he can about the group. Such questions as these are pertinent: Is this the group's first meeting? Are the members likely to know one another? Is the meeting one of a series? If so, what has happened at previous discussions? How

much do group members know about the discussion method? How much do they know about the topic? See Chapter 3, pp. 25–27, for additional suggestions.

2. *Explaining the discussion method.* This is necessary the first time a group meets, or when a new method is to be used. Members don't like to play before they know the rules of the game. For the first meeting, prepare a mimeographed "program" giving the topic, the names of group members if they are known, and these "do's and don'ts":

a. Remember that discussion is a cooperative venture in serious conversation. It succeeds best when anyone feels free to join in at any time. Help the leader keep the discussion moving forward.

b. Listen thoughtfully to others. Be sure you understand them before you reply. Ask for explanations when you need them.

c. Speak when you can contribute something to the discussion, but don't monopolize it.

d. Under usual conditions, don't speak more than a minute at a time.

e. If you don't understanding something, say so; perhaps there are others who don't understand it either. Ask for an example.

f. If you disagree with what is said, say so frankly, but in a friendly way.

g. Don't wait to be called on, especially at the beginning of the discussion.

h. Remain seated while speaking and address other members informally.

i. Come to the meeting with the intention of taking part. If you don't have information, you can at least ask questions.

j. Don't expect an important question to be settled in one discussion. Perhaps your opinions need unsettling.

3. *Securing information.* Providing adequate information, written in laymen's language, that presents both sides and different points of view, is often a real problem. Those who prepared the Fund for Adult Education's series of film-discussions, "Great Men and Great Issues," and "World Affairs are Your Affairs," meet the situation by supplying a short film and an objective essay for each program. Members are supposed to read

the essay before the meeting. For the Great Books discussions, each member reads the same section of the same great book. Some teachers of courses in discussion methods or human relations employ collections of "cases," or reports of situations involving the interactions of people, as the basis for class discussions. A recent collection, suited to this purpose, is *Customs and Crises in Communication* by Irving J. Lee (Harper & Brothers, 1954).

These examples do not meet the needs of those who gather to discuss current controversial issues. Propaganda organizations are often eager to supply information supporting their point of view. This should be used only when the source is clearly indicated. If given sufficient warning, the local library may gather materials from various sources. So may the extension division of your state university. On local issues, members of your group may interview those who have different sources of information and those who have different opinions. This is the method of the cooperative investigation. As group members gain experience, they will require less help from the leader in gathering evidence.

4. *Planning ways of starting discussion.* If group members are familiar with the discussion method and each other, the leader may need to do little more than state the topic, comment on its importance, raise a question, and rely on someone to answer it. However, if the group members know little about taking part in informal discussions, and especially if they know little about the topic, the leader should plan some way of getting the meeting off to a good start. These methods (some of which have been mentioned) have been used successfully to avoid that awkward pause following the leader's opening statement when everyone waits for someone else to say something:

a. Distribute brief items of information to be read at the beginning of the meeting.

b. Ask members who have had firsthand experiences related to the topic to speak for two minutes at the end of the leader's opening statement.

c. Provide a member with a short "situation story" illustrating the problem, or how it was dealt with elsewhere, to be read at the proper place in the discussion.

d. Have two or three members ready to act out, in three or four minutes, a scene illustrating the problem.

e. Occasionally the introduction may be built around a map, graph, or picture.

f. Prepare a list of True-False statements about the topic if the purpose is to check the accuracy of the members' information.

g. Prepare a list of Agree-Disagree statements designed to draw out the members' opinions and beliefs about the topic.

In using the last two methods the leader explains that the purpose of the tests is to find out what members know or what they believe about the topic and that they are not to sign their names. Each member can score his own information test; for the opinion test the leader can simply ask how many agree with each statement and how many disagree.

The most common fault of introductions in group discussion is their length. The leader takes too much time saying that members should be brief and concise.

5. *Preparing a discussion outline.* Although the informal group discussion proceeds with a minimum of organization, the leader should have an outline to guide the conversation. The leader's outline should not be a strait jacket but a guide; if he occasionally wishes to announce its three or four main topics in advance, the group should feel free to suggest changes, but the chances are that any well-prepared outline will be accepted, even though the discussion may depart from it. The typical outline for an informal and impromptu discussion consists of a series of questions which the leader can throw out to stimulate the thought of the group and to direct it along somewhat logical lines. Knowing that some of the questions will not impress the group, the leader usually prepares more than can be fully considered. He will also realize that the discussion, once started, may take an unexpected turn, compelling him to make up a new outline as he goes along. Even should this happen, some plan is better than none.

Most discussions should focus not only on a specific problem but also on one particular phase of it. It is possible, however, to set up a general outline that can be adapted to various problems. Such an outline, based on the normal steps in thinking through a problem, is given below. The discussion need not always begin with the first step in this general outline. It should begin at the point the members have reached in their thinking.

GENERAL DISCUSSION OUTLINE

I. What is the nature and extent of the problem?
  - A. What background information is necessary to an understanding of the problem?
  - B. What is the specific question to be decided?
  - C. How serious is the problem?
  - D. What factors must be considered in deciding on a solution?

II. What solutions are proposed?
  - A. What are the advantages of each proposed solution?
  - B. What are the disadvantages?

III. What is the group's initial reaction?
  - A. On what points does the group substantially agree?
  - B. What are the chief differences?
    1. On matters of fact?
    2. On matters of opinion?
  - C. How fundamental are these differences?

IV. Which solution, or combination of solutions, seems best?
  - A. Can a compromise be reached that will meet with general approval?
  - B. If not, which solution, after debate, is favored by a majority?

V. How may the chosen solution be made effective?
  - A. What can this group do?
  - B. What can I do?

Here is a sample outline on "What can we do about death on the highway?" It was prepared for a group already familiar with the nature and extent of the problem. It began, therefore, at the stage of examining possible solutions. The leader phrased it in questions. He was prepared to break the outline down into even smaller units or to omit some parts if they failed to interest the group.

SAMPLE DISCUSSION OUTLINE

I. *Nature and extent of the problem.*
   A. Two-minute summary of information gained at previous meeting.
   B. Can anyone add anything to this?

II. *Where can we begin to tackle this problem?*
   A. How about teaching safe driving in our high schools?
   B. How can we approach our adult drivers? What about men's luncheon clubs and women's organizations?
   C. What about our local traffic laws? Are they adequate?
   D. Are we getting proper enforcement of our local traffic laws?
   E. Can anyone suggest still other ways of reducing traffic accidents?

III. *What steps should be taken?*
   A. Can we agree on what ought to be done to meet this problem? What seems the best place to begin?
   B. What can this group do?
   C. What can we do as individuals?

B. CONDUCTING GROUP DISCUSSION

1. *Getting the meeting started.* Start it on time. Use one of the methods suggested in the preceding section. The leader's opening sentences should set the style of the conversation by their brevity and directness. He should then ask a question he thinks most likely to start discussion. If this fails, he should ask another.

2. *Defining the question or topic.* Sometimes the first thing is to discuss what certain key words mean and to agree on how they are to be used in the discussion. Such words as *propaganda, socialized medicine, delinquency, free speech, discrimination, the American way,* mean different things to different people.

3. *Keeping the discussion on the track.* The tendency of discussion to ramble from the main road creates one of the leader's most perplexing problems. If he lets the discussion wander wherever chance remarks may take it, he is no leader; if he holds too rigidly to his outline and appears to dictate the course of the conversation, the members will feel that it is not a genuine

group enterprise. This is a problem in finding the golden mean. The good leader is reluctant to announce that the discussion is off the track; he might have to reverse himself if members point out relationships that have not been apparent to him. The best procedure is to ask whether the discussion is on the subject and let the group or the speaker of the moment decide.

4. *Making occasional summaries.* The leader has a better "bird's-eye view" of the course of the discussion than others in the group. He should use summaries during the discussion for any or all of three purposes: (a) checking needless repetition, (b) bringing a random conversation back to the subject, (c) recording apparent areas of agreement or disagreement. He should exemplify the purpose of summaries by making them brief, impartial, and in the language of the group, and by resisting the temptation to magnify disagreements or to assume agreement when none exists. He can insure accuracy and lack of bias by asking the group to check him or to add points he has overlooked. Some leaders ask the *content recorder*, or secretary, to provide summaries.

5. *Encouraging general participation.* It is not essential that everyone talk at a discussion meeting, but it is important that anyone with something to say be encouraged to say it. The leader must make it easy for people to talk. He should not merely terminate his introduction by saying, "Well, now you know what the problem is. Does anyone have anything to say?" The least he can do to encourage participation is to act and speak as though he expects it.

Ordinarily it is a mistake to single out a member for a pointed question. If he has nothing to say at the moment he may be embarrassed and even less likely to speak up when he does have something on his mind. Timid members may be drawn into the discussion by asking them for specific information the leader knows they have. He may secure broader participation by inquiring whether those who haven't spoken would like to comment, and by recognizing those who have kept silent but look ready to speak rather than more vocal group members. Or he may make a statement and ask how many agree with it, using the visible responses as an excuse to ask reticent members why they agree or disagree.

6. *Keeping the discussion from becoming one-sided.* Ordinarily the leader should enter the discussion only to ask clarifying questions, bring discussion back to the subject, summarize, make transitions to the next point, or to interrupt the long-winded speaker. However, in spite of the leader's plans for an impartial discussion, those who speak may support the same point of view. Minority members, feeling that their views are unpopular, contribute to the one-sidedness by their silence. The leader must then specifically invite opposing arguments. He may introduce them himself, or he may quote opposing authorities and ask, "What do you think of these arguments?" These are artificial devices, but their use is justifiable. The leader must not let the discussion become a propaganda meeting.

Members of a discussion group, realizing that the leader has made some investigation of the topic, often ask him questions as an "expert." He should be reluctant to assume this role; he may sometimes further the discussion by stating facts if he is sure of them, but he should never give his personal opinion without labeling it as such. The best procedure is to turn such questions back to the group, letting the answers come from members whenever possible.

7. *Getting at the root of the matter.* Discussion leaders are rightly concerned lest their group chat pleasantly, voice casual opinions, and never get at the real problem. A meeting in which everyone talks and reaches a unanimous conclusion may not be a good discussion. Members may not give their real beliefs. Unless they have studied the problem, their conclusions may be based on insufficient evidence. They may substitute rationalization for reasoning.

What to do? Obviously, the leader must not attempt to force his conclusions on the group. When, however, he feels that the discussion is not getting below the surface, he should attempt by probing questions to call attention to the lack of evidence, the evasion of the basic issues, or the weakness in reasoning.

8. *Remaining in the background.* How can the leader do all the tasks we have assigned him, and remain in the background? The answer lies primarily in his ability to make suggestions instead of giving directions, to ask questions instead of answering them. The leader can learn to phrase his questions so he

keeps attention focused on others, even though he speaks more frequently than any group member. In a 30-minute radio discussion with 5 participants, the leader spoke 43 times; Mr. A, 17 times; Mr. B, 21 times; Miss C, 16 times; Mr. D, 15 times. This is an average of four "speeches" a minute. The leader can remain in the background only if he keeps his questions and comments brief.

Leaders sometimes phrase their questions so that a "yes" or "no" answer will suffice. In most cases this tends to stifle discussion; when a man says "yes," he agrees but is not inclined to say more. Occasionally, however, this type of question may be useful simply to get an expression of opinion to provide the basis for discussion; even the one-syllable answer may focus on a point no one has previously discussed.

Rhetorical questions that imply an answer do not stimulate group thinking; questions that are too broad baffle the members. Make the questions pointed and specific. Start with "what" to get opinions and facts, "who" or "where" for sources of opinions and facts, "why" for reasons and causes, and "how" or "when" to narrow the discussion and get down to specific cases.

One obvious way for the leader to remain in the background is to encourage group members to share the responsibility of leadership. Whenever a member helps keep the discussion on the track, volunteers a summary, or questions the information or evidence, he is taking the spotlight off the leader. But if one member does all these things, he would focus it on himself and seem to be taking over the leader's duties instead of helping him.

9. *Concluding the discussion.* The two most important bits of advice are: conclude when the time announced for adjournment has arrived; and conclude with a summary. Some groups have a content recorder to give the summary; more frequently, in informal discussion, it is given by the leader. It should include the major issues discussed, the pro and con arguments, the major agreements and disagreements. He should resist any temptation to hand down conclusions.

The summary should reflect a consensus only if there is real agreement, and give fair coverage of divergent views. This can best be done by using tentative language, subject to correction by group members, or to revision based on further conversation:

"Apparently we agree that. . . . When we tried to apply the policy, however, we found at least two points of view. . . . Some believed that . . . others argued that. . . ." After the summary, the members should have the opportunity to offer suggestions or corrections.

A good summary will send the members home with the feeling that they have made progress, though in most cases they will not have completed their analysis of the subject. This is the time to ask group members whether they wish to devote another meeting to the problem.

10. *Evaluating the discussion.* Until group members are familiar with the discussion method, the last ten minutes of the meeting should frequently be devoted to an evaluating session. A number of evaluation procedures are explained in Chapter 6. The leader may conduct this session, raising pertinent questions to call attention to the discussion's strengths and weaknesses. When the group has had some experience with discussion three or four group members may be assigned to answer such questions as: Did the discussion stay on the track? If not, why not? How many members spoke? Did any try to dominate the meeting? Was the evidence sufficient in quality and quantity?

The evaluation may be done by a team consisting of the leader, a content recorder, whose duties are described in the preceding section, and a process observer. The observer notes such things as the nature and extent of participation, the way the leader functions, the dead spots in the discussion, and the morale of the group. To avoid hurt feelings, he rarely singles out individuals for adverse criticism. Rather, he points out weaknesses in the procedure, and suggests, often in question form, the cause and cure of these weaknesses. Members may decide for themselves whether the shoe fits.

III. The Role of the Committee Chairman

The prospective committee chairman should read the preceding section on the leadership of group discussion. Much of what is said there applies equally to the chairmanship of committees. But not all. There are significant differences, both in the purposes and procedures of the meetings and in the qualifications for leadership. Committees are usually smaller, are always composed of members of a single organization, and have a definite assignment that may require a series of meetings extending over weeks or months. These factors affect the nature of the meetings and the chairman's part in them.

The differences in the qualifications for leadership are even more important. The committee chairman should be selected as much for his knowledge of the problem under investigation as for his mastery of discussion methods. In legislative assemblies, the chairman, through length of service, frequently becomes an authority on matters that come before his committee.

A. PREPARING FOR THE COMMITTEE MEETING

The committee chairman's first official duty is usually to call an organization meeting. Because committee sessions are often long, all that has been said about the comfort and informality of the surroundings is especially important. If the members are not acquainted, some type of social gathering should precede the business sessions.

In preparation for the first meeting the chairman should (a) get a copy of the legislation creating the committee so that he will know the nature and extent of the assignment, (b) draw up a tentative outline of the work required to complete the project, and (c) learn as much as he can about the interests and abilities of each committee member. The outline should not, of course, be announced to the committee. Quite the contrary. It should be given as a suggestion for consideration by the committee. In many cases individuals will be appointed to investigate different phases of the problem. The information the leader obtains about committee members will be useful in making these assignments. The chairman should be willing to do his full share of the work and to study aspects of the question that do not interest other members.

B. CONDUCTING COMMITTEE MEETINGS

Committees sometimes fail because members come to their task with their minds already made up and spend their time defending their conclusions instead of listening to others. The chairman in his opening statement should invite members to join in a cooperative search for the best answer to the problem. This applies most directly to deliberative committees.

At the first session, a secretary should be chosen to summarize the discussion and record any tentative conclusions that may be reached. These reports serve the same purpose as the leader's summaries in informal group discussion. Actual voting on the report should be deferred to the last committee meeting. Excepting the motion to adjourn, the motion to adopt the committee report is the only formal parliamentary action required of the committee.

Committee meetings should be informal. The chairman joins in the discussion on equal terms with other members. He should not, however, use his position to dominate the discussion or to sell his ideas. He should see that the committee keeps working toward its goal, and that courteous attention is given to each member and each proposal.

Here is a general outline of parliamentary procedure for committees appointed to study an important problem and submit recommendations for action. It assumes that subcommittees will be appointed to conduct different phases of the investigation and that several meetings will be required to complete the assignment. In most cases, however, a much simpler agenda will suffice. The procedure should fit the task.

1. Call meeting to order: roll call. (Choose secretary at first meeting.)

2. Committee objectives: purpose and scope of assignment.

3. Establishment of committee procedure; appointment of subcommittees.

4. Analysis of problem, including "movable" and "immovable" factors, i.e., those about which something may or may not be done.

5. Establishment of minimum essentials of any acceptable solution.

6. Examination of possible solutions.

7. Evaluation of proposed solutions according to item 5.

8. Reports of subcommittees.

9. Decision: committee action.

10. Choosing method of presenting committee report.

11. Preparing and presenting report.

12. Evaluation of committee procedure for future action.

13. Adjournment.

Most committee meetings are not open to the public, and most of the time the public doesn't care. Other members of the organization can speak when the committee report is presented. On important questions, however, the committee members frequently want to get the public's reaction as a part of their investigation. In that case they may hold public hearings, where citizens and their spokesmen are invited to express their opinions. The public hearing is described in the next chapter.

Members should not commit themselves, especially on controversial matters, until they have completed their study. Then any differences of opinion should be openly recognized and frankly discussed. It is to secure the values of vigorous discussion of committee reports that legislative bodies require representatives of the minority party on deliberative committees. If differences of opinion among committee members are not resolved, majority and minority reports may be made to the parent organization. The committee report is usually given by the chairman, who explains it and moves its adoption. He may call on others to present and defend sections of the report with which they are most familiar.

IV. The Role of the Conference Chairman

The chairmanship of a conference is often the most exacting assignment confronting a discussion leader. Especially is this true when the objective is to settle a dispute, but even when there is no hostility among the delegates there is the problem of getting them to work together. The opening sessions may well require all the leader's skill, plus tact and willingness to make haste slowly.

Conferences to settle active disputes offer both the greatest challenge and the greatest difficulty, especially when the delegates have no experience with the discussion method. The difficulties are greatest when the conflict has reached the "fighting stage," with each side announcing its demands and denouncing the opposition. Then even the best leader or moderator may be able to do little until there has been a "cooling off" period.

The United States Conciliation Service notes three stages in labor-management relationships: the organization stage, the fighting stage, and the cooperative stage. This agency believes that the fighting stage can generally be eliminated if a conference is held when the first signs of a dispute appear. To that end it offers the services of skilled conference leaders. The advice to confer about disputes early applies equally to relationships among community groups. The leadership of local conferences will usually be drawn from the community.

A. Preparing for the Conference

1. *Calling the conference.* We are describing here conferences called to consider a local problem. Such conferences do not just happen. Some person or group must sense the need and be willing to do a good deal of preliminary planning. The person who takes the lead may be called the organizer to distinguish him from the chairman, who is usually chosen at the first session. If the organizer belongs to one of the participating groups, others may feel that he and his organization want the lion's share of the credit for the enterprise. This may be avoided by forming a voluntary committee, with representatives of various groups, to participate in the planning and join in issuing a "call" for the conference. The call should include the reasons for the project, a statement of the problem, the bases for inviting organizations and selecting delegates, and a tentative outline of the program. The tentative nature of the outline should be emphasized. Conference members may wish to amend it as the discussions progress, but even in its preliminary form it gives invited organizations a basis for deciding whether they wish to accept, and if so, the type of delegate that will best represent them.

2. *Determining the size.* The purpose of the meetings and the number of organizations interested in the problem should determine the size of the conference. Although it is true that not more than twelve or fifteen people can think together efficiently without a tendency for the less vocal members to become an audience, it is equally true that other considerations often make it advisable to invite a much larger number of delegates. Conferences to settle specific disputes are usually organized in multiples of three, representing equally the two parties in controversy and the public, with nine or twelve as the maximum member-

ship. Conferences for other purposes, and with larger numbers of delegates, are described in the next chapter.

3. *Creating the right atmosphere.* Conferences often bring together some who are not acquainted and some who dislike each other. Much depends on what happens before the first business session. These suggestions have proved helpful:

a. If possible, delegates should be housed in the same hotel, taking their meals and recreation together. What happens between sessions may be fully as important as the meetings.

b. Hold the sessions on neutral grounds so the host-guest relationship will not put either side at a disadvantage.

c. Begin the conference with a luncheon or dinner. Arrange place cards so delegates from an organization will not sit together. People find it harder to hate each other after they have eaten together.

d. Arrange the conference room so hostile groups do not sit on opposite sides facing each other. If the group can be seated at a round table, no one can complain that he is seated at the foot and his favorite enemy at the head.

B. Conducting the Conference

1. *Electing chairman and secretary.* The first order of business is the election of a chairman and a secretary. Groups not familiar with the conference method often fail to distinguish between the work of the conference chairman and that of the presiding officer at a public meeting, who may be chosen for the prestige he lends to the occasion and who often does little more than announce the musical numbers and introduce the speakers.

The conference organizer usually knows more than anyone else about the purpose and plan of the meetings. If he is equally informed about discussion methods and skilled in their use, he is the obvious choice for the chairmanship. In the interests of efficiency the conference chairman should preside at all sessions. But, to avoid hurt feelings, it may be advisable to rotate this office, though the thought process is interrupted while the group gets acquainted with the new moderator, and he gets acquainted with his task.

The secretary, who is usually not a delegate, should be able to prepare a ten-minute objective summary of a two-hour session to be read at the opening of the next one. These summaries are for the guidance of the group, not for publication. All formal voting on conference findings should be postponed until the last session. This avoids the necessity of rescinding actions that no longer seem wise.

2. *Adopting a tentative schedule.* At the proper point in the first session the chairman should invite discussion on the tentative outline included in the call for the conference. The delegates might be encouraged to adopt the general plan with the right to amend it as the situation warrants.

Here, for example, is a general outline, prepared by the United States Conciliation Service, for labor-management conferences called to consider grievances:

Step   I. What is the grievance (or dispute)?
Step   II. What are points of agreement and disagreement (dividing the latter into the less controversial and the more controversial questions)?
Step III. Discussion of the less controversial points.
Step IV. Discussion of the more controversial questions.

With these steps as a foundation for the conference, it may be hoped that the group will be able to arrive at a satisfactory solution.

The following stock outline should be used in building the plan for any conference dealing with a controversial issue:

Step   I. Locating and defining the problem
Step   II. Exploring the problem
Step III. Examining suggested solutions
Step IV. Choosing the best solution
Step   V. Planning to secure its acceptance

The outline for "educational" conferences will have a different emphasis. Here most of the time may be spent in exchanging information and points of view. The result should be a better understanding of the problem. The delegates may then, either as individuals or as representatives of their groups, urge that the needed action be taken by the proper agencies.

The procedure at these conferences should be that of the

informal discussion or committee meeting. The chairman's role is that of the discussion leader or moderator, not that of the committee chairman. He must be sensitive to the feelings and prejudices of delegates and willing to spend what seems a disproportionate amount of time in getting them acquainted and in building good will. He must convince everyone with his fairness and his desire to follow the facts, wherever they may lead. And, when he has done his best and the conference still does not seem to get anywhere, he should remember that often the results are not immediately apparent. The meetings may have started the process of forming a public opinion that will result in action later.

C. DISCUSSION IN INDUSTRY

We hear a great deal about discussion in settling labor disputes, but too little about its other uses in industry. These other uses are growing in scope and importance. Three factors are at least partly responsible: (a) The desire to give labor some voice in management, thereby improving morale; (b) the realization that communication between the main office and the shop, and among employees, is frequently defective, thereby lessening efficiency; (c) the discovery that workers will often learn from each other more easily than from an outsider, thereby lessening the need for special teachers.

In his book, *Conference Methods in Industry* (Harper & Brothers, 1949), Henry M. Busch says that the conference method has proved its value in developing company policy, solving technical problems, disseminating information, explaining directives, improving communications, clearing up misunderstandings, and training employees. Busch's definition of the conference is broad enough to include the informal group discussion, the committee, and the panel, as well as the conference.

Foreman training, says Busch, is now on "the conference basis in the largest, most progressive industries. Most foremen have experience in every kind of shop problem. By sharing their experiences they can aid each other, and perhaps increase the production level of the shop." They can share their experiences more effectively in conversation than in any other form of communication. Directives from the main office are often needlessly involved, written in main-office language that the foreman and his crew neither speak nor fully understand. Face-to-face conversation offers the shortest, clearest road to understanding, provided the group members know they can speak freely, without danger of reprisal by superior officers.

The duties of the industrial conference chairman closely resemble those of ordinary group discussion.

V. Parliamentary Rules in Discussion

Some writers on discussion are sharply critical of parliamentary procedure. Witness these assertions: "Parliamentary rules have functioned for years to stymie meetings." They "have made it possible for a few to take control . . . under the dead hand and habit of Mr. Robert." "Certain tricks of parliamentary procedure are favorite weapons for confusing issues and creating doubt. . . ." "The rules for discussion should be almost the complete opposite of *Robert's Rules of Order.*"

These writers do less than justice to Mr. Robert who wrote in *Parliamentary Practice*: "One who is constantly raising points of order and insisting upon the strict observance of every rule in a peaceable assembly in which most of the members are ignorant of these rules and customs, makes himself a nuisance, hinders business, and prejudices people against parliamentary law. Such a person is either ignorant of its real purpose or else willfully misuses his knowledge." We note in passing that ignoring parliamentary rules does not inevitably result in good discussion.

But the fact that rules can be misused does not mean they should be abolished. Robert says ". . . if each member could talk on any subject as long as he pleased and as many times as he pleases, and if all could talk at the same time it would be impracticable in most cases to ascertain their deliberate judgment on any particular matter." Parliamentary rules are just as necessary, and no more technical, than rules governing baseball or football.

The main objectives of parliamentary rules are: to guard against hasty, ill-considered action, to give each member an equal right to speak, to determine the will of the majority, and to protect the rights of the minority. Hence these sensible rules for discussion in *business* meetings:

1. Only one question can be considered at a time. It must be properly phrased, moved by one member, seconded by another, and then thrown open for discussion and debate. Similarly, only one amendment can be considered at a time.

2. No one can speak until he has risen, addressed the presiding officer, and been "recognized."

3. No one can speak a second time on the same question as long as another wants to speak for his first time.

4. When two or more members rise to speak, the chairman should recognize one who opposes the preceding speaker, and preferably one who has not spoken previously.

Those who criticize parliamentary procedure seemingly overlook the distinction made by Robert and others between rules for committee meetings and those for business meetings of large organizations. Committee meetings are usually quite informal, as we have indicated earlier. Members do not rise and address the chair. They can speak as often as they please provided they do not deprive other members of opportunities to present their views. The chairman may take an active part in the discussion. He may put questions to the vote on his own initiative after an informal discussion. "In all cases," says Robert, "efforts should be made to obtain a unanimous report." If members of an organization wish to consider a question informally, some one moves that they meet as a "committee of the whole" for a specified period and purpose. Non-controversial matters may be passed by unanimous consent.

Parliamentary procedure is the best method yet devised for taking action on controversial issues. There are rules for hastening action when something must be done immediately. There are also ways of delaying action for various valid reasons. Then, in our form of government, there comes a time when legislators must stand up and be counted. The will of the majority, sometimes two-thirds of those present, becomes law. The minority must abide by the decision while leaders of the "loyal opposition" lay plans to reverse the decision at the next session. The same procedure, adapted to the needs of the group, applies to our clubs and organizations: the secretary's minutes, when read and approved, are the legal record.

These generalizations may be helpful in determining the degree to which parliamentary rules should be followed in business meetings of clubs and organizations. Greater use should be made of parliamentary procedure when the group is relatively large, when the purpose is action rather than exploration, when the division of opinions is sharp, when a relatively high degree of formality is desired, and when members of the group are familiar with parliamentary rules. When the converse of these conditions is true, there should be less reliance upon formal, or parliamentary, procedure. For a handbook adapted to the needs of discussion groups see *Essentials of Parliamentary Procedure* by J. Jeffery Auer (Appleton-Century-Crofts, Inc., 1942).

5.

The Leader of Public Discussion

A PUBLIC DISCUSSION TAKES PLACE BEFORE AN audience. The program begins with a conversation or speeches by invited speakers and is usually followed by a *forum* in which audience members question the speakers, give additional information, or state their own opinions on the topic.

Much of what we have said about leading group discussion also applies here. But not all. Large meetings must be more formal, so audience members can see, hear, and follow what is going on. The leader needs more skill in speaking; he must speak loudly enough to be heard. He must be able to attract and hold the attention of the audience, especially during the forum period. While small discussion groups may be content to move slowly, and to explore interesting bypaths, larger audiences grow impatient if the meeting drags and does not seem to be getting anywhere.

In this chapter we describe the leader's role in six types of public discussion: the panel, the symposium, the public hearing, the debate forum, the lecture forum, and such combinations of group and public discussion as institutes, conventions, and semipublic conferences.

I. Preparing for Public Discussion

To avoid repetition, we describe here the leader's duties that are similar for all, or nearly all, types of public discussion.

A. Choosing the Speakers

Someone, usually a program committee, must make the usual arrangements for public meetings. The chairman or moderator should either be a committee member or be consulted about the choice of speakers. He should urge that the following criteria be followed as closely as possible:

1. The speakers need not be widely recognized authorities on the topic, but they should know considerably more than the audience does. And they should not be afraid to say, "I don't know."

2. On controversial topics, speakers should believe in the point of view they are to present. Possible exceptions occur in debates where the teams are assigned to present the strongest pro and con arguments, and in the lecture forum when the speaker attempts an objective survey of the issue.

3. To avoid bias, speakers should have about the same degree of prestige.

4. For the same reason, speakers should have about the same skill in public speaking.

B. Briefing the Speakers

The chairman or moderator should supply the speakers with information on the purpose of the meeting, and a description of the expected audience. In many cases the speakers are not familiar with discussion and naturally want to know what they are supposed to do. On this point, the experience of those who conduct radio discussions is helpful. The University of Chicago Round Table is a panel without a present audience. Each speaker is provided with a booklet describing the program and listing a number of "do's and don'ts." Panel members chosen for their knowledge of the topic, and well in advance, meet a day or two before the broadcast to agree on a general outline. The morning of the broadcast, they have a long meeting, filling out the outline, deciding who will introduce each topic and how much time should be devoted to it. This done, they make and listen to a rehearsal recording of the discussion.

America's Town Meeting of the Air is our best known example of the symposium or debate forum. It is held before studio audiences ranging from a few hundred to several thousand. While the length of the broadcast has varied and with it the number and length of speeches, the general procedure remains the same. Speakers read prepared statements of a specified length. The moderator and speakers have an impromptu discussion lasting five to eight minutes. The remaining time is devoted to questions from the audience. The speakers meet to read their speeches and are asked to be available the rest of the day for revision of speeches, voice recordings, and final plan for the broadcast.

The lecture forum may not require as much advance preparation, but the chairman should be sure the speaker knows the time limits and the procedure during the forum period.

C. Briefing the Audience

Audience membership should know when, how long, and how often they may speak. Otherwise they will do nothing for fear of doing the wrong thing. The best method of furnishing this information is to prepare a mimeographed program for distribution as members arrive for the meeting. The program should include: the discussion topic; the names of the speakers and their qualifications to discuss this topic; the time schedule for the meeting; the rules for the forum period; and a blank space in which the audience members can take notes and phrase questions for the forum period. It may also include such things as definitions and technical terms, outline maps or charts, and statistical data—important information that is hard to present in short speeches.

Here is a suggested list of rules for listener participation in the forum. It should, of course, be modified to fit the topic and the occasion.

YOUR PART IN THE FORUM PERIOD

1. The most frequent types of audience participation in the forum are: (a) requests for further information, or an explanation of some point; (b) requests for a speaker's opinion; (c) friendly questions allowing the speaker to amplify or explain a strong argument; (d) challenging questions directed at weak spots in a speaker's argument.

2. You are not limited to asking questions. You may add information to that presented, state your own beliefs, or oppose opinions expressed by the speakers.

3. The time limit for speeches should not exceed two minutes (about 300 words); one minute is better. It gives someone else a chance to speak.

4. Make a brief outline of your speech and write out your question. Be sure that what you have to say is relevant.

5. When you wish to speak, rise and be recognized by the chairman.

6. Don't ask permission to speak a second time as long as others who have not spoken are seeking recognition.

7. While you are talking to the moderator or a speaker on the platform, speak loudly enough so audience members in the back seats can hear you.

8. Avoid name calling. Intelligent people can discuss each others' ideas without discussing each other.

D. PLANNING THE FORUM

Perhaps the most important test of a moderator's skill in presiding at public discussions is his success in geting active, interested participations in the forum period. Obviously, only a small number of those present can get the floor to speak. But active listening is participation, and a speaker may make a point or ask a question that most of those present want answered. The uncertainty as to what will happen and the opportunity to cross-examine a speaker stimulate active listening.

The process of briefing the listeners, described in the preceding paragraph, is a first step in planning the forum period. The moderator should also see that the purpose and procedure of the forum are described in advance publicity. In addition, he may do these things:

1. *Plan questions in advance.* If the audience is not familiar with the discussion method, or the topic, the moderator may take steps that would otherwise not be necessary. He may give pertinent questions to audience members for use if the forum starts slowly or at the end to make sure that the discussion concludes on a relevant and important point. He may also distribute items of information about the topic to make sure that the supply of information is both adequate and accurate.

2. *Plan to handle problem situations.* There are three kinds of individuals who talk too much: those who talk easily and know a great deal about the topic; those long-winded members who don't realize how long they have spoken; and the irrelevant person who always tries to speak on his pet theory. The best way to handle long-winded speakers is to state the time limits before the meeting begins and stop the first one who tries to speak overtime. There will be irrelevant speakers as long as there are muddled individuals. The best the moderator can do, short of ruling them out of order, is to ask them to connect what they are saying with the issue under discussion.

More troublesome, though less frequent, are forum speakers who indulge in name calling, attacking persons rather than arguments. Such individuals ignore the basic assumption that intelligent people can discuss each other's ideas without discussing each other. An occasional personal remark should probably be ignored. But if a member persists in their use, the moderator has no other choice than to rule such remarks out of order.

E. Special Techniques

Several techniques have been devised to secure active participation in the forum period. Three of the most promising are: role playing, the case method, and "Discussion 66."

1. *Role playing* as used in discussion is the spontaneous acting out of problems or situations. It adds variety to the discussion and may portray a situation more vividly than can usually be done by straight description. The actors are told to give the opinions and portray the actions of the characters they represent. They are given a few minutes to agree on the points they should make; beyond this, there is no rehearsal. The acts should not exceed four or five minutes and may be used either to start the forum or to illustrate a point if interest lags. When used to illustrate a problem situation, two or three role-playing groups may, in effect, test different solutions.

The moderator must make sure the actors understand the nature and purpose of their assignment. They must resist the temptation to give caricatures that raise laughter or are merely entertaining. They must have self-confidence and willingness to enter wholeheartedly into the act. When well done, role playing creates interest and stimulates discussion. When poorly done, it might better have been left undone.

2. *The case method* also presents specific situations or problems to stimulate discussion, but does not rely on their impromptu presentation. The moderator may write descriptions of typical cases and have them read to the audience if discussion lags.

If projecting equipment is available, pertinent data of various kinds can be prepared on slides or filmstrips for use in starting the forum discussion. An enterprising director of foreman training secured a portable tape recorder and prepared a series of short episodes, each showing a right and wrong way of meeting a troublesome situation. While these devices are not suited for large audiences, they can be seen or heard by groups of 150 to 200 people, if the seating can be properly arranged.

3. *"Discussion 66,"* popularized by J. Donald Phillips of Michigan State College, gives each member of the audience a chance to state his opinion on some phase of the discussion topic during the forum period. The technique is also referred to as the "buzz session." The audience is divided into groups of six, either by arranging the chairs, if they are movable, or by combining three members in one row with the three seated just behind them. There is, of course, convenience but not magic in the number six; five to eight may do as well.

Each group chooses a chairman and a secretary-spokesman, who is provided with a 5- by 8-inch index card, containing a carefully worded question on which judgment is sought. The chairman urges each member to state his opinion. The secretary records the opinion, but not the name, of each member on the card. The chairman then asks the group to choose what the members regard as the best answer, which is also recorded on the card. For relatively small public discussions, the secretary-spokesmen give oral reports as soon as they reassemble in general session. For large meetings, the written reports are summarized for later presentation.

The name "Discussion 66" suggests that six members discuss the questions and come to some conclusion in six minutes. Even if the time spent in organizing the group is not included, one can do little more than record existing opinions or first impressions in six minutes. The technique is not so well adapted to the earlier stages of analyzing a problem that is new to the group. When the topic is a familiar one, however, some moderators have used the "buzz session" before the formal presentation, to help formulate an agenda, or to focus on specific questions which the listeners hoped the speakers would answer in due course.

A representative of the American Telephone and Telegraph Company who observed "Discussion 66" in action in a forum with 180 supervisors of the Michigan Bell Telephone Company was most enthusiastic about it. It revealed to management questions that were troubling the employees. "The anonymity of the questioner is a vital factor." Without doubt questions were raised which would have been unasked if an individual had to stand up and ask them. The plan ought to be useful in "developing the upward flow of two-way communication between management and labor." But it should not be used unless management is willing to answer all questions frankly.

II. Leading a Panel Discussion

We assume that panel members, about equal in prestige, have been chosen for their knowledge of the topic and their skill in public conversation. We hope that they will neither attempt to dominate the meeting nor remain silent unless they are questioned directly. They should present different points of view or different types of information. The leader should do his best to avoid a biased presentation of controversial issues.

A. Briefing the Members

The leader should hold a planning session well in advance of the public meeting. He should explain the purpose of the discussion, and present the following rules:

1. There are no formal talks. The method of public conversation is used throughout the meeting.

2. Individual contributions to the conversation should be brief. Four 30-minute Northwestern Reviewing Stand broadcasts, in 1949, had 71, 73, 87, and 91 separate "speeches," ranging in length from three to about two hundred words.

3. Address your remarks to each other, but speak loudly

enough so those in the rear of the room will hear and feel included in the conversation. In this respect, you have the same problem that confronts the actor.

4. You must listen as well as speak. Show by your facial expression and manner that you are paying attention to other panel members. You can hardly expect audience members to be interested if you and your colleagues seem bored or indifferent.

5. Don't sit back and wait to be called on. If two of you try to speak at once, the leader will decide who is to speak first.

6. If you have three points to make, label them, "1, 2, 3."

7. Sometimes direct your remarks to another panel member: "Jones, what would you say about this situation?" or "I'll have to disagree with you, Smith. . . ."

8. Help establish your colleagues (and yourself) as authorities on the question: "Jones, you're our expert on labor relations, . . ." "From your ten years in China, Brown, what conclusions . . .?" "I speak as the only fraternity member on this panel."

B. Preparing an Outline

The rest of the planning session should be devoted to an informal discussion of the topic. The leader notes the points made and the proofs advanced by each member. From these he makes an outline to be considered and approved before the meeting adjourns. He agrees to expand the outline and send a copy to each member. The panel should hold a brief session just before the public meeting to recheck the outline and to agree on a plan for getting the discussion off to a good start.

Below is a sample outline for a discussion of the housing problem. Note that it gives an approximate time allotment for each subtopic and the name of the member who is to introduce each point.

WHAT CAN BE DONE ABOUT NEW HOUSING IN MIDDLETOWN?

Participants: Brown, Smith, Jones
Total time: approximately 36 minutes

I. *Introduction* (not over 5 minutes).

A. Conversation recently overheard (Jones).

B. Results of Chamber of Commerce survey of present housing (Smith).

C. Future development of community depends upon new housing (Brown).

II. *Is the principal need for privately owned homes or for rental property?* (about 8 minutes).

A. Depends upon who needs housing (Smith).
   1. Professional people and Main Street merchants generally expect to be permanent residents and want their own homes (Jones).
   2. Factory employees, less certain of permanency, would prefer to rent desirable apartments and houses (Brown).
B. This questions also depends on income levels; data from Chamber of Commerce survey (Smith).
C. But, most of all, it depends upon the cost of home building (Brown).

III. *What has happened to housing costs?* (about 8 minutes).

A. Costs have skyrocketed; give figures comparing today with ten years ago (Jones).
B. Summarize effect of housing costs on the desire for new housing: this means little hope for the building of as many new homes as Middletown needs (Brown).
C. Effect of higher costs on building apartments and other rental property (Smith).

IV. *What are the possible answers to this problem?* (about 12 minutes).

A. Prefabricated housing is a possibility (Brown).
B. Possible modifications of trade agreements and trade-union policies which have kept costs high (Smith).
C. Attraction of idle investment capital into apartment building (Jones).
D. Alteration of building codes to lower costs and retain health and safety standards (Smith).
E. Government assistance and latest public housing developments (Brown).
F. Opening new surburban developments for lower land costs (Smith).

V. *Summary* (3 minutes). All three, with Jones last.

Panel members often ask whether they should rehearse the

discussion. If they do, the program may lack spontaneity; if they don't, it may lack substance. The director of the University of Chicago Round Table concludes that "preparation including rehearsal is the necessary basis of spontaneity."

C. Preparing a Program

The leader should see that a program is prepared for distribution as audience members arrive. It should contain the question for discussion, the names and qualifications of panel members, and the rules governing audience participation. It may also include definitions, summaries of proposed plans, and statistical data that the listener can consult during the discussion.

D. Getting the Meeting Started

When a program containing this information is in the hands of the audience, the leader can begin with a sentence or two about the nature and purpose of the topic and ask a question to start the discussion. Each panel member should get into the conversation within the first two or three minutes. The audience is just as impatient when the leader spends too much time getting the discussion under way as it is with a slow first act in the theater.

E. Keeping the Discussion Going

Since each panel member has a copy of the outline, the discussion is not likely to wander off the track. The leader's main duties are to keep the conversation moving from point to point, to see that each panel member has a chance to express his views and to ask questions intended to clarify points for the audience. On rare occasions he must break up disputes between panel members.

The leader should try to draw the panel members into the discussion equally. Thomas Fansler gives this report of the number of contributions by a seven-member panel:

Mr. A	Mr. B	Miss C	Leader	Miss D	Mr. E	Miss F
17	23	26	49	1	12	6

There were 66 contributions from the leader's right, only 19 from his left. He spoke too often in an attempt to keep the discussion going.

Three veteran members of the University of Chicago Round Table gave this advice to panel members, which, if followed, would provide valuable help for the leader:

"We learned quickly not to emphasize what somebody else is adequately emphasizing."

"My strategy is to play up what others play down . . . to give a balanced picture out of our joint participation."

"We make no pretense of trying to give full information on any specific point of view, or to reach any definite conclusions."

"You cannot cite long statistics. You cannot use technical terms without defining them explicitly."

"If one of us makes a *faux pas*, another will invariably say, 'You mean thus and so,' and make it possible to smooth it over."

"The excellence of the spontaneity depends in large measure upon the intensity of preparation."

F. FROM PANEL TO FORUM

In any public discussion the formal presentation should rarely take over half of the meeting time. To say it another way, at least 40 per cent of the program should be reserved for the forum.

When the panel has used its share of the time, the leader, with or without a summary of the main points, invites the audience to enter the conversation. He should make it clear that listener participation is not limited to asking questions. Members should be invited to give additional information, and to agree or disagree with the opinions of panel members.

The meeting should end with some sort of summary. Its content would depend on whether the purpose of the discussion was to supply information or to suggest solutions to a problem. If there is a content recorder, he should make a summary statement, after which the leader asks whether the panel wishes to offer additions or corrections. The leader frequently makes the summary with the same invitation to panel members. Or the leader may ask each panel member to make a hundred-word summary of his own position on the question. After these statements, the leader should add points that have been overlooked.

III. Presiding at a Public Hearing

Public hearings are designed to maintain two-way communication between the citizens and their government. Legislative committees hold public hearings on proposed legislation. Administrative agencies, varying in scope from the Federal Communications Commission to the local school board, hold hearings to explain their plans and test public reaction to them. Special committees may use public hearings in the course of investigating a situation that may or may not require legislative action. While hearings conducted by legislative committees consider the merits of a bill or resolution, those held by investigating committees begin with an analysis of the problem.

Some public hearings resemble the symposium; sometimes they are more like the debate. The seating arrangement in the more formal hearings is suggested in the diagram.

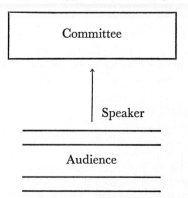

While the speaker addresses his remarks to the committee, he also hopes to impress the listeners whose reactions may in turn influence the committee.

The chairman may have gained his position through seniority; he may, or may not, know a great deal about the bill under consideration. Having stated the nature and purpose of the meeting, he usually calls first on the author of the bill, then on those who favor its passage and, finally, on those who oppose it.

Speakers usually are asked to state the organization they represent. On important matters where many wish to speak, they must register a request to appear, so the committee may schedule a series of meetings.

The hearings may last for days or weeks. In such cases, the practice of hearing all who favor the bill before the opposition can speak may not serve the public interest. Those who attend a meeting or two are likely to hear only one side of the case. The remedy for this problem is to alternate pro and con speakers.

The chairman and committee members may question the speaker during, or at the conclusion of, his speech. They may ask for further information, question the value of evidence, or criticize the speaker's conclusions. Depending on the attitude of the committee toward the speaker or the bill, the questions may be friendly or hostile. Hearings are no place for a poorly prepared speaker or one who loses either his head or his temper during cross-examination. This is why business and professional organizations employ skilled speakers to represent them at hearings.

While the chairman may, and often should, join in questioning speakers, his participation should be that of the investigator who is trying to discover the facts, not that of the partisan. He is largely responsible for the tone and temper of the meetings. Ordinarily, he need do little advance preparation. If, however, he thinks one point of view is being neglected, he may suggest that the committee invite speakers to present it. He may also, in conference with majority and minority leaders, agree on a time allotment for each side. In that case, the leaders accept the responsibility of deciding who shall speak and for how long. Since there is no forum period, the chairman simply announces that the meeting is adjourned after the last speaker has finished.

IV. Moderating a Symposium

The participants in a symposium are a moderator and from two to four speakers, each of whom speaks for a specified time on an assigned phase of the topic or problem. This type of meeting may be used either to provide information from different sources or to consider the merits of different solutions. The symposium provides more information, and if the speeches are properly integrated, a more unified consideration of the problem than are easily obtained from the panel. Knowing the spotlight will be on them for a specified number of minutes, the speakers are more likely to make careful preparation. The symposium is essentially a public speaking program; the panel is essentially conversational. For this reason, the symposium is the better method for large audiences.

The preparations for the symposium include:

a. deciding the purpose of the meeting
b. choosing and framing the topic to arouse interest
c. choosing speakers
d. choosing a chairman
e. briefing chairman and speakers on the objectives and procedures

Some of these steps are self-evident; here we consider how the general advice in earlier chapters applies to this type of discussion.

A. Choosing the Speakers

Speakers should be chosen by a program committee, in consultation with the moderator. Speakers should be selected for their prestige, knowledge of the topic, and skill in public address. Unless they are regarded as thoughtful, well-balanced individuals, who can speak with some degree of authority, people will not come to hear them. To avoid bias, the committee should choose speakers with about the same degree of prestige, knowledge of the topic, and speaking skill.

The speakers chosen should be willing to spend some time in preparation. Those who attend have a right to expect well-organized speeches, expressed in layman's language. The speakers should remember that there are distinct limits to what an attentive listener can learn in eight or ten minutes. Excellence in speaking is, of course, desirable. However, listeners will excuse lack of skill in delivery if they feel the speaker has something he really wants to say and is doing his best to say it effectively.

B. Preparing an Outline

When the problem is new, the symposium should be designed to supply information about it. Each speaker should present information from a different source or on a different phase of the question. Here is a typical outline and time schedule for a 70-minute symposium of this sort:

Topic—What is our present system of providing medical care?

	Minutes
Chairman—Introducing topic and speakers . . .	3
Speaker A—The private practitioners . . .	8
Speaker B—State and federal health services . . .	8
Speaker C—Commercial health and accident insurance . . .	8
Speaker D—Cooperative group health plans . . .	8
Chairman—Introducing forum period . . .	2
Forum—Audience questions and comment . . .	30
Summary—Chairman or content recorder . . .	3

If, however, the audience is fairly familiar with the problem, the symposium should consider what can be done about it. Here is a short outline for a discussion of juvenile deliquency. Speaker A brings the audience up to date on the problem. (The same time allotments can be used.)

Topic—What can we do about juvenile delinquency?
Speaker A—What is the present problem?
Speaker B—What can be done by home, school, or church?
Speaker C—What can be done by juvenile courts?
Speaker D—What can be done by welfare agencies?

C. Briefing the Speakers

Whenever possible, the moderator should arrange a briefing session soon after the speakers are chosen. If they cannot meet, the moderator should send them a description of the symposium and names of their partners. The speakers should understand that discussion means "thought in process," that their purpose is to help listeners analyze the problem, not to announce conclusions to them. Each talk is a step in the process of analysis. The briefing should include agreement on time limits of speeches and procedure during the forum.

D. CONDUCTING THE SYMPOSIUM

Following the briefing session, the moderator should prepare a program including: a statement of the discussion topic, the list of subtopics, the names and qualifications of speakers, time limits, and rules on participation in the forum period. This program should be distributed to audience members as they arrive for the meeting. It guides both speakers and listeners, and enables the moderator to get the discussion under way in two or three minutes.

The moderator's introductions should focus attention first on the program, then on the speaker's qualifications as an authority. In preparing his introduction, the moderator should avoid two extremes. He should not be content with the general remark that "Mr. X. needs no introduction. He is a recognized authority in his field." On the other hand, the introduction need not tell the life story of Mr. X. Here is the introduction of the first speaker on America's Town Meeting of the Air, May 26, 1953:

"Mr. Young, a student at Harvard, who has studied in China and in Paris, was a teacher at Harvard before he entered government service and served in the Air Corps during the war. He has been a State Department Far Eastern Affairs expert almost since the war ended. And now to the subject, 'What is the future of Japanese-American relations?" Here is Kenneth D. Young."

E. FROM SYMPOSIUM TO FORUM

Various devices are used to bridge the gap between the speeches of the experts and questions or comments from the audience. The moderator may arrange with one or two persons to ask questions as soon as the invitation is given. Or the speakers may question each other to point up important issues. Or a panel from the audience may go to the platform to question the speakers.

With a large audience and a short forum period, listener participation is often limited to asking questions. It is difficult to avoid a miscellaneous set of questions that scatter over the subject or a one-sided series of questions directed at one of the speakers. To deal with these situations, the moderator may ask for questions on various aspects of the problem, or for questions directed at different speakers. If these are not forthcoming, the moderator should himself direct questions at neglected issues or neglected speakers. Or he may ask all speakers to comment on each question if they care to do so.

To make the best use of the forum period, questioners should make their questions brief and concise, and speakers must resist the temptation to extended answers. To avoid ending the forum on a weak or irrelevant note, the moderator may arrange to have someone ask an important question on a neglected issue a minute or two before adjournment.

The Town Meeting broadcasts conclude without a summary, perhaps to emphasize the fact that the purpose is to stimulate further study. If a summary is desired, each speaker may be given a minute for that purpose, or a content recorder may be appointed.

V. Moderating a Debate

The debate is a kind of symposium which inevitably occurs when people with different beliefs study the same problem and arrive at different conclusions. Debate is also a school exercise in which members of affirmative and negative teams, speaking alternately, urge the adoption or rejection of the affirmative resolution. In "real-life" debates, speakers may not function as teams. Thus, one speaker may oppose the United Nations because he believes it has too much power; another, because he believes it has too little.

Some discussion enthusiasts charge that debating is bad because it focuses attention on differences, thereby increasing the difficulty of reaching a consensus. They charge further that debates are likely to be unduly contentious. This isn't necessarily so. The criticism is valid only when debaters take positions on the question before they study it. And contentiousness is not inherent in debating. It may be found in discussion.

A. Choosing the Debaters

The usual standards should be applied: the debaters should be approximately equal in prestige, knowledge of the problem, and speaking skill. They should understand that the purpose of the meeting is to present an analysis of the problem and a fair presentation of the arguments on both sides. A more thoughtful, though less dramatic, debate may result if extreme partisans on both sides are not chosen. However, more people are likely to attend a debate between those partisans.

B. ORGANIZING THE MEETING

The chief characteristic of debate is that it provides equal opportunity for affirmative and negative presentations. Here is a time schedule for a debate with four speakers.

	Minutes
Moderator: Opening statement about problem	3
Speaker A: Favoring proposed solution	8
Speaker B: Opposing it	8
Speaker C: Favoring it for different reasons	8
Speaker D: Opposing it for different reasons	8
Forum: Audience participation	20–25
Speaker B or D: Negative summary	3
Speaker A or C: Affirmative summary	3
Total	60–70 minutes

A three-speaker arrangement may be used for shorter debates. The first speaker gives background information and states the issues; the second and third speakers present the pro and con arguments. Theodore Granik, moderator of the American Forum of the Air, has developed a thirty-minute "dialogue-debate." He secures two speakers who differ, sometimes rather intensely, on a hot issue, introduces them, asks a question, and sits back to see what happens. He enters the conversation to ask another question, rap for order, or clarify a point. The debate closes with a one-minute summary by each speaker.

In one of these debates, Mr. Granik spoke 23 times; Speaker A, 57 times, and Speaker B, 55 times. On six occasions the debaters spoke at the same time. Of Granik's participations, 13 were recognition of speakers or transitional phrases, 6 were questions or comments intended to clarify points, and 6 were questions designed to keep the discussion moving.

C. Conducting the Debate

The duties of the moderator in arranging and conducting the debate are the same as for the symposium. The program, in addition to information on the topic, the speakers, and the procedure, may include a ballot on which listeners record their evaluation of the program and their beliefs on the question.

VI. Presiding at a Lecture Forum

The lecture forum is the easiest to arrange and the most frequently used type of public discussion. In an uninterrupted talk of thirty minutes, the lecturer can make a more orderly analysis of the problem than is usually possible in conversational discussions. The lecture forum can be used for audiences of all sizes. But it has definite limitations. A speaker who has studied a problem sufficiently to qualify as an authority usually has formed an opinion as to the proper solution. He naturally finds it difficult to present other solutions fairly.

A. Choosing and Briefing the Speaker

The ideal discussion lecturer combines knowledge of the problem with knowledge of the discussion process. He must be willing to help his listeners analyze the problem, instead of advocating his conclusions. He must be patient with those who ask unimportant or irrelevant questions. He must resist the temptation to answer every question with a speech.

A special briefing session may be unnecessary. However, the chairman should make sure the lecturer knows the nature and purpose of the meeting, the probable size of the audience, and how much the listeners know about the problem. There should be agreement on the length of the speech and the procedure during the forum.

B. Planning for Audience Participation

Observers generally agree that it is difficult to get discussion in the forum period, especially when there is large audience. Mary Ely, of the American Association for Adult Education, attended 75 lecture forums and in only six found what she regarded as genuine group thinking. Instead, there were miscellaneous questions about the lecture. Audience members hesitated to challenge the speaker's conclusions. Speakers sometimes yielded to the temptation to embarrass such questioners. Miss Ely concluded that the forum is important for its effect on both speakers and listeners. Knowing that his information may be questioned and his opinions challenged, the speaker prepares carefully and adjusts his speech to his audience. Knowing that they may question or challenge the speaker, the listeners pay close attention to his speech.

The method known as "Discussion 66," described earlier, has been used to give everyone in the audience a small part in the meeting. In addition, the following suggestions have proved helpful:

1. Audience participation will improve in quality and quantity if the lecturer ends his speech with a question or two in place of the usual summary or appeal to action.

2. If the lecturer does not do this, the chairman may ask a series of questions that will direct attention to the main points of the speech.

3. When the lecturer advocates one solution or point of view, that fact should be made clear. To keep his presentation from being entirely one-sided, the chairman may have other points of view presented briefly during the forum. Or he may arrange to have the other side, or sides, presented at another meeting. Some chairmen invite the speaker to take a seat in the audience after his lecture, on the theory that this will encourage more discussion among audience members, and less reliance upon the question-and-answer pattern.

C. CONDUCTING THE MEETING

The chairman should open the meeting with a two- or three-minute talk, stating the importance of the topic and the lecturer's qualifications to discuss it, explaining when and how audience members may join in the discussion. During the lecture he should note questions he may ask if audience members do not.

The chairman may use an audience panel to make the transition from the lecture to the forum. This panel consists of three or four audience representatives, chosen before the meeting. At the conclusion of the lecture, they go to the platform. The chairman leads them in a discussion of the speaker's main points and then invites audience members to enter the conversation. The time schedule should be about as follows:

Chairman's opening statement	3 minutes
Lecture	30 minutes
Audience panel	10–15 minutes
Forum	15–20 minutes

In opening the forum, the chairman should announce that questions should be questions, not little speeches with a question mark on the end, and that the time limit for speeches from the floor is one minute. During the forum, the chairman may have to enforce the time limit, help an audience member to phrase his question, repeat a question so audience members can hear it, ignore a member who wants to speak more than his share, and rule out personal or irrelevant questions. When the time for adjournment approaches, the chairman should announce that fact and use whatever procedure has been agreed upon for closing the meeting.

VII. Leadership in Combinations of Group and Public Discussion

Recently there have been various attempts to use discussion in the programs of *institutes, conventions, work conferences,* and *workshops.* Some references to such programs have been made. We will include here some instances in which there are general sessions and sectional meetings, even though the meetings may not be "public" in the sense that everyone is invited to attend.

A. INSTITUTES AND CONVENTIONS

The *Institute for Education by Radio-Television* meets annually at the Ohio State University and is open to anyone who pays the registration fee. The three-day program in 1952 included four symposium forums at general sessions, nineteen "work-study groups," and eleven "special interest groups." The leaders of these special groups, with the assistance of a secretary, prepare a summary of the discussion for inclusion in the "Proceedings" published under the title *Education on the Air*. The same discussion leader presides during the forum period at all general sessions.

The programs of professional conventions and various types of annual meetings follow the pattern of general sessions and sectional meetings, though with less use of group discussion. It is impractical to provide 40 trained leaders and meeting places needed to divide 1000 registrants into groups of 25 for informal discussion. Aside from an occasional use of "Discussion 66," the symposium is most frequently used for general sessions; the panel, for sectional meetings. And sometimes the word "discussion" seems to mean something to do if the speakers finish before adjournment time.

B. WORK CONFERENCES

The "work conference" is described in Chapter 4. When the number of delegates is large enough to require a number of work groups, the general sessions tend to use procedures applicable to public meetings. The type of conference we have in mind lasts at least two days. It opens with a general session to state the nature and importance of the problem, and to describe the discussion procedure. General sessions are usually held every half day to hear reports from the various groups and to propose possible solutions. The conference closes with a general session to take whatever action seems justified. Descriptions of three such conferences appear in the February, 1948, issue of the *Adult Education Bulletin*.

Teachers College, Columbia University, reports an experiment in training discussion leaders to participate in a conference on problems involved in teaching reading (*Teachers Prepare for Discussion Group Leadership*, by Corey, Halverson and Lowe, 1953). The conference committee planned a half-day program beginning with a panel discussion by teachers representing various grade levels, followed by twelve small group discussions including the entire school staff. A full-day training session was provided for the twelve teachers chosen to lead the group discussions.

The basic material for the training session was a tape recording of eight brief, simulated discussion episodes on the following leadership problems:

a. Beginning a meeting
b. Building the agenda
c. Dealing with the excessive talker
d. Handling conflict within the group
e. Keeping things moving
f. Keeping on the beam
g. The dominating leader
h. Closing the meeting

The episodes, two or three minutes in length, illustrated good and bad leadership practices, and ended with questions raised by the narrator. These questions were then discussed with the director of the training session as leader.

Evaluation forms were filled out by the trainees at the conclusion of the training session and again after they had led the discussion on reading problems, and by 180 members of the teaching staff who were members of the small discussion groups. At the end of the training day, 9 leaders rated it as "very valuable," 3 as "quite valuable." After they had led the discussions, all 12 rated the training as "very valuable." Of the 180 members of discussion groups, 31 per cent rated the discussion as "very adequate;" 54 per cent as "quite adequate."

The duties and responsibilities of leaders in combinations of group and public discussions are the same as for other similar types of meetings.

C. WORKSHOPS

Ronald Lippitt reports (*Training in Community Relations*, Harper & Brothers, 1949) a ten-day workshop, combining the study of a community problem and research in discussion methods. The problem concerned ways of combating racial and religious discrimination. The planning committee included members wanting help in solving the problem, specialists in discussion methods, and social scientists interested in evaluating methods and results.

There is space for only a brief description of the discussion leadership. The 49 workshop members were divided into three discussion groups. The workshop was in session 86 hours in ten days. Of this time, 38 hours were spent in meetings of the entire group; 38 in small group meetings; 8 in spontaneously organized meetings; and 2 in testing. The membership of this group, including the leader, remained constant throughout the workshop.

In the small group discussions Group A averaged 161 participations per hour; Group B, 243; and Group C, 160. Leader A was responsible for 66 per cent of the participation in his section; Leader B, for 65 per cent; Leader C, for 70 per cent. This table shows the *percentage* of his time each leader devoted to different activities.

	Leader A	Leader B	Leader C
Starting and coordinating discussion	48	68	56
Giving information	23	10	17
Present, but on sidelines	22	13	23
Absent, group member in charge	4	2	1
Caretaker of group routines	3	3	1
Taking role in sociodrama	6	3	2
Mediating group conflict	0	1	0
	100	100	100

Here is the percentage of time the average work group spent on various activities: group planning, 19; listening to lectures, 1; discussing the problem, 31; reality practice and discussion of it, 41; miscellaneous and routine activities, 8.

6.

Evaluating Discussion

THE DISCUSSION IS OVER, THE MICROPHONE IS dead, and the janitor has turned off the lights. What have you accomplished? And what can you do better at the next meeting? In this chapter we offer some observations on what you can and cannot expect from a discussion, and some ways of evaluating the results of discussion meetings.

I. Objective Studies: What You Can Expect

As we indicated earlier, recent years have seen a good deal of experimentation with discussion, as a technique for the classroom, as a tool for implementing the democratic process, and as a means of improving human relations. Objective studies have been reported in professional journals. What follows is a brief summary of their findings and a comment on the implications they hold for the average discussion meeting.

1. In a number of investigations involving judgment it has been found that the average of the group judgment is superior to most individual judgments; those of a few individuals, on the other hand, were always better than those of the group. This would appear to mean that several heads are usually better than one.

2. From other studies we learn that group thinking, resulting from some form of discussion or consultation, is superior to individual thinking whenever these factors are important: a variety of points of view on a problem, a large number of suggestions for the solution of a problem, or a large number of effective criticisms of the solution proposed. It has also been

found that in the discussion of problems involving a number of steps, groups do not err as often as the average individual. This suggests that in discussion, if not in cooking, the more cooks and the more recipes the better the broth.

3. In various experiments it has been found that a group is more likely to accept good suggestions advanced in discussion than to reject them; more likely to reject bad suggestions than to accept them. This seems to allay any fear that discussion groups may be stampeded to accept hasty and ill-conceived conclusions.

4. In other studies it has been found that in discussion groups those individuals who have "right" answers to a problem tend to hold to them more tenaciously than do the individuals who have "wrong" answers. This suggests that wrong-minded people are not likely to dominate group thinking and sway their colleagues to wrong conclusions.

5. In further experiments it has been found that members of discussion groups are more likely to feel personal responsibility for decisions than are audience members or those who are told what to do. This seems to indicate that taking part in decision making through discussion helps to insure follow-through.

6. In many studies it has been found that even comparatively short discussions may change the opinions or attitudes of as many as 40 per cent of the listeners. Such changes may be in various directions if the problem has several alternative solutions. This appears to demonstrate that discussion is an effective device for stimulating individual thinking.

7. Finally, experimental evaluations of numerous discussion training programs, in and out of classrooms, demonstrate that those being trained do make substantial changes in their behavior with groups, and become more effective leaders and participants in discussion. Thus we conclude that discussion leadership is a skill that can be acquired through study, observation, and practice.

II. Misconceptions: What You Should Not Expect

While these research studies indicate the values of discussion, its limitations should also be made clear. Some of these were stated in Chapter 1. Here we consider some common misconceptions that must be understood if we are to avoid being disappointed in the outcome of discussion.

1. *Agreement is no sure test of success.* Too often it is assumed that if people just talk things over they will become as agreeable as lovebirds. The extent of agreement is assumed to measure the value of the discussion. But good discussions may be held in which people disagree, often vigorously. Indeed, when agreement on a controversial subject comes too easily, the group may have been thinking superficially, or members may have avoided points of disagreement. In the latter case, the real discussion takes place when people gather in small groups after the meeting. Discussion is for open minds, and it may be successful even when they do not all close together.

2. *There may be "silent" participation.* It is sometimes thought that the success of a discussion may be measured by counting the number who said something. This assumption overlooks the fact that listening is an active process, that intelligent listening is participation. One person speaks and group members who are paying attention are "talking back," formulating ideas into sentences that may be spoken if they get a chance. Everything the attentive listener hears is accepted or rejected by him, whether or not he speaks up so that others may hear him. In public discussions only a small proportion of those present can speak. But all can participate by listening, and learn from those who do speak.

3. *Discussion may not "settle" anything.* It should not be assumed that every discussion will settle the problem at hand. Indeed, the aim is sometimes to unsettle people so they will do some thinking about the problem. Until a problem has been clearly isolated and defined, pertinent facts and opinions gathered, and alternative solutions considered, we have not gone far enough in the thought process to take final action. More than one discussion may be necessary to reach this stage. When we do, we count the votes and follow the judgment of the majority.

4. *Even small groups are important.* Americans like statistical information. We measure yield per acre, tally runs per inning, and judge performance by the applause meter. It is unfortunate, but understandable, that people often measure the success of a

meeting by the number in attendance. Yet we would hardly evaluate a debate in the United States Senate by the number of visitors in the gallery. The personnel of a group may be more important than its size. And the attitudes of participants may reveal more than their numbers. Information gained and opinions formed in discussion meetings may be passed from person to person until they affect the thinking of a whole community

III. Criteria of a Good Discussion

Few leaders have the opportunity to evaluate single meetings under the controlled conditions of experimental studies. But all can "take stock" after each meeting by using some of the types of information listed below as criteria.

1. *Attendance records.* We have just said that size alone may not be an important measure of a meeting. An average attendance of twenty would be plenty for a discussion group. The same figure would suggest failure for a series of public forum meetings. Whatever the size, if the attendance steadily decreases, the series is hardly successful, and those in charge should take note.

2. *Nature and extent of participation.* An experienced leader, or a trained observer on the discussion team, can judge whether group members participate freely, keep their contributions relevant, and sustain their interest throughout the meeting. One observer may keep a chart, showing how many members speak, and how often, whether there is genuine group discussion or a series of two-man dialogues. He may also analyze individual contributions and estimate their quality. Later in this chapter we suggest procedures for keeping such records, and for conducting a self-evaluation period at the close of the meeting. The leader and the observer can also, in a series of discussions, judge the behavior of group members toward those holding contrary opinions. Is there an increased willingness to listen to the other fellow's point of view? Is there a decreased tendency to indulge in personalities and name calling? Is there less inclination to be dogmatic? Is there increased skill in making relevant contributions to the discussion?

3. *Changes of attitudes toward the problem.* The leader may

evaluate the discussion by the changes of attitude toward the problem. We describe more fully procedures for measuring these changes, indicating whether members have formed new attitudes, shifted those previously held, or strengthened their initial beliefs.

4. *Individual or group action.* This test is whether the discussion has changed individual behavior, or culminated in group action. The results, in either case, may not be immediately apparent. Following a discussion of the advantages of home ownership it may be months or years before a convinced member may be able to buy a home. On the other hand, a discussion of the values of church membership, or Community Chest needs, may result in immediate action. Committees and business meetings usually deal with matters requiring group decisions. Here the leader may inquire whether the discussion provided information needed to formulate a solution to the problem. Some discussions, it should be remembered, are held only to exchange information; in such cases it may be impossible to observe individual or group action other than the process of sharing ideas.

5. *Postmeeting conversations.* Participants often report that the best discussion took place after the meeting adjourned, and people gathered in small groups to continue talking informally. If those who attend continue the discussion at home, over the luncheon table, or at the office, weeks or months later, the meeting was a success. But if people are anxious to adjourn, seem to be interested only in getting home, and speak only of matters unrelated to the topic, the attendance at the next meeting will likely be smaller. A questionnaire which gives those present an opportunity to evaluate the discussion and suggest topics for future meetings is one way of applying this test. Sample questionnaires are suggested later in this chapter.

6. *Expressions of outside interest.* A whole chain of community events may be set off by even a small meeting. Other groups may discuss the problem; it may be the subject for newspaper editorials or letters to the editor; a minister may preach about it; or school children may want to talk about it in class. These developments indicate the success of the original meeting. When their interest is aroused, members of discussion groups are apt to want further information about the problem, and

their friends may also. Bookstores and libraries may supply the evidence for this measure of the effectiveness of a discussion.

IV. Measuring the Results of Discussion

Discussion aims at arousing interest in a problem, but it also has one of these purposes: to supply background information, to form or change attitudes, or to secure action. An information test is a simple measure of effectiveness when a discussion is intended to provide a factual basis for further meetings. The test may be given both before and after the discussion to distinguish what was learned from what was already known. If the purpose is to secure action, simple observation will give the answer. To measure the effectiveness of discussion in forming or changing attitudes, however, requires one of these special techniques.

A. THE SIMPLE BALLOT

A vote on a single question or statement is the easiest method of measuring attitudes: "Do you support the proposed bond issue to build a community center?" or "America should adopt a policy of free trade." Audience members are asked to write "Yes" or "No" on slips of paper, but not to sign their names. This precaution is important; individuals feel free to state what they honestly believe and can change their opinions without letting their neighbors know about it. Though easy to use with large groups, the simple ballot fails to measure accurately the effects of a single discussion; the voter has no chance to register a weakening or strengthening of his original opinion unless it changes his vote.

B. THE SHIFT-OF-OPINION BALLOT

This technique overcomes the weakness of the simple ballot; it permits the voter to record opinion changes smaller than a shift from one side of the question to the other. On the opposite page is a sample ballot used in one of a series of discussions on "How can the buyer get his money's worth?"

Though this type of ballot does not give the listener an opportunity to express his reactions to various arguments advanced on the central question, it does provide some basis for

skilled persons to construct the tests or conduct the interviews. Those who are interested in these specialized techniques can find full descriptions in some of the references listed at the end of this book.

V. Methods of Evaluating Group Behavior

In an earlier chapter we spoke of the values of discussion for the individual participant. Leaders should want to know whether these values were realized. They should also make inquiries about the way the discussion was conducted. Discussion Evaluation Form No. 1 is a simple one to be filled in by members at the close of a meeting.

Responses to Form No. 2 may be even more helpful in evaluating specific aspects of a public discussion, such as one which begins with a symposium (or a panel, lecture, or debate), and uses a "buzz session" to open the forum period.

Additional information about individual behavior and reaction may be provided by the more detailed questionnaire in Form No. 3. In preparing evaluating forms it must be remembered that some people will not take the time for thoughtful consideration of too many questions.

Discussion Evaluation Form No. 1

Your considered answers to the following questions will be helpful in improving our future meetings.

1. What is your over-all reaction to this meeting? Circle one number:

    0   1   2   3   4   5   6   7   8   9   10

    Extremely   Neutral   Extremely
    unfavorable   favorable

2. What do you think were the weaknesses in this meeting?

3. What do you think were the virtues of this meeting?

4. How would you suggest that the next meeting be improved?

Discussion Evaluation Form No. 2

1. Please give your over-all reaction to this meeting. Check one:
   ___Very successful   ___So-so   ___ Rather unsuccessful
   ___Rather successful   ___Very unsuccessful
   Please give the major reason for the reaction you checked above:

2. What was your reaction to the symposium? Check one:
   ___Very good   ___So-so   ___Rather poor
   ___Rather good   ___Very poor
   Please give the major reason for the reaction you checked above:

3. What was your reaction to the forum "buzz session"? Check one:
   ___Very good   ___So-so   ___Rather poor
   ___Rather good   ___Very poor
   Please give the major reason for the reaction you checked above:

4. How did this meeting correspond with what you expected? Check one:
   ___Very similar   ___So-so   ___Rather different
   ___Rather similar   ___Very different
   Please give the major reason for the reaction you checked above:

VI. Techniques of Evaluating Individual Participation

We have emphasized the role of the process observer in evaluating the nature of individual contributions. He, or other members of the discussion team, will need some techniques of record keeping to make this evaluation.

1. The simplest device for determining *frequency of participation* is to have one observer keep a tally of the number of participations by each member. He should count not only complete statements, but also such attitude-revealing interjections as "That's right!" "No!" or "What do you mean?" A refinement of this procedure is to use a different symbol in the tally

Discussion Evaluation Form No. 3

Your answers to these questions will be helpful to those in charge of planning future meetings. Please be frank. Check the answer in each case which most nearly fits your reaction.

1. Was the subject for discussion of interest to you?
   ___very interesting; ___mildly; ___not at all.
2. Did you learn something new about the subject?
   ___a good deal; ___a little; ___nothing.
3. Do you now have a better understanding of the subject?
   ___much better; ___somewhat better; ___no better.
4. Was the meeting as a whole a worthwhile experience?
   ___very worthwhile; ___moderately; ___not at all.
5. Did the leader (or formal speakers) talk
   ___too long? just long enough? ___not long enough?
6. Did you think the forum period was
   ___too long? ___just long enough? ___not long enough?
7. Did you take part in the discussion (or forum period)?
   ___more than once; ___only once; ___not at all.
8. Will you come again?
   ___yes; ___perhaps; ___no.
9. What suggestions would you make for improving this meeting?

10. What subjects would you like to discuss at future meetings?

to indicate those participations which are general statements or questions addressed to the whole group, as contrasted with those addressed to some particular member. This same observer may also ask each member, at the conclusion of the discussion, to write down on a slip of paper the names of three other members who he feels contributed most to the discussion. A tabulation of these individual judgments may be compared with the frequency tally to determine whether there is any apparent correlation between quantity and quality of participation.

2. A record of the *flow of participation* begins with the construction of a seating chart, with a small circle drawn on a large sheet of paper to represent the position of each member. After the leader's opening remarks a line should be drawn from

his circle to the one representing the next person to speak, then a line from that circle to the next speaker, and so on. The result should be a "spiderweb" diagram. In order to keep the diagram from becoming too cluttered, and also to determine whether the pattern of participation changes as the discussion progresses, several observers may take turns, starting a new chart at five- or ten-minute intervals. It is useful to number each of the lines representing a participation, in order to have a record of sequence. Evaluations of the evidence provided by flow charts are suggested by these questions: Do most of the lines converge upon the leader, or is there a fair amount of "cross talk"? Are the most loquacious people sitting close together, and the relatively silent ones also? Does the diagram reflect real *group* discussion, or a series of little monologues or dialogues?

3. One technique for observing the *nature of participation* is to make up a chart listing the name of each member, and also each of the possible "member roles" described in Chapter 2.

Group-functioning roles	*Problem-solving roles*	*Negative roles*
Morale builder	Inquirer	Dominator
Conciliator	Contributor	Blocker
Compromiser	Elaborator	Cynic
Expediter	Reviewer	Security seeker
Standard setter	Evaluator	Lobbyist
	Energizer	

The observer may then check under the appropriate heading his classification of each contribution of individual members. The resulting data will provide a profile or composite picture of each individual's role in the discussion. A simpler procedure for recording these data, but less discretely, is to classify each individual participation as "group-functioning," "problem-solving," or "negative." In either case the observer must be skilled in identifying quickly each contribution in terms of these "member roles" or some other set of labels he may devise.

4. Observers may employ a variety of techniques for judging the *value of participation*. The simplest is to tally the contributions of each member by evaluative symbols: + for significant, objective, or clarifying contributions; ○ for contributions of moderate value; − for contributions of little or no value. More

precise labeling of contributions is obtained by using additional symbols, such as C for "committee work," comments such as re-phrasing, clarifying, defining, or summarizing; Q for questions; T for tangential or irrelevant remarks. In any case the observer may also wish to ask group members for their evaluations of each other (unsigned lists when in written form) on questions such as: "Which three members of the group contributed most to the outcome of the discussion?" "Which three members had the greatest influence on your own thinking about the problem?" "Which three members would you most like to have take part in future discussions?" or "Which members showed the greatest improvement in discussion skill?"

The extent to which any of these techniques for evaluating individual participations should be used will depend upon the nature of the group and the purpose of the discussion. Learning groups, in or out of the classroom, will be most concerned with information helpful in improving future discussions. Groups that work together over long periods, such as many committees, will profit from individual participation evaluations, especially in early meetings. Those meeting for one time only, such as many conference delegates, are less likely to be concerned with this kind of information.

Those with considerable experience in observing and evalu-ating individual participation in discussion submit these ad-monitions:

a. No one method of evaluation should be used over and over. The effectiveness of any one will lessen after it has been used two or three times.

b. No technique of evaluation is effective unless it is applied by an observer who can translate the results into meaningful and specific suggestions for improving discussion procedure.

c. Reports of individual evaluations must be made, publicly or privately, in ways that will strengthen the group without making any member feel insecure.

d. Constant emphasis upon evaluations inclines some mem-bers to say nothing, rather than risk saying the wrong thing, and others to focus more upon procedures than products of discussion.

Appendix A

Projects for Discussion Leaders

WHEN WE WROTE THE FIRST EDITION OF THIS handbook we assumed that it would be used largely by present or prospective leaders of discussion meetings. We discovered, however, that it is also used in short courses for adult groups and to supplement the text in college courses where a more extensive treatment of discussion is desired.

This fact suggested the desirability of including exercises and projects to serve the needs of adult discussion leaders and of students in discussion classes. To serve these dual purposes, we prepared the following projects. Some are designed for the individual leader; others for the members of discussion groups; still others for students in regular credit courses. While each project is keyed to certain pages in the text, we do not assume that they should be undertaken in this order, or that any leader, group, or class will use all of them.

Project 1

If equipment is available, record sample programs of such radio series as America's Town Meeting of the Air, University of Chicago Round Table, Northwestern Reviewing Stand, Invitation to Learning, or American Forum of the Air. The prospective leader can listen to find out how the professional leader: (a) gets the discussion under way, (b) keeps it from straying too far from the topic, (c) gives each speaker an equal chance, (d) moves the discussion from one point to the next, (e), deals with problem members, (f) concludes the discussion.

He will probably want to listen to the recording two or three times to observe all of these points. (See pp. 68–80.)

This may also be used as a group project. Members may be assigned to observe what each speaker does: how often he speaks, how much information or evidence he contributes, whether he listens to other speakers, whether he is cooperative or otherwise, etc. The members' observations and opinions should be presented in a forum period.

Project 2

If recording equipment is not available, get three or four copies of a network discussion, or one of equal quality. This is also a dual purpose project. The leader-in-training can study the script for at least partial answers to the questions raised in the preceding project.

The transcripts may also provide the program for a discussion meeting. Members, after a rehearsal or two, read the discussion to the group. The forum period should begin with comment on the discussion method and devote what time is available to a discussion of the problem, or topic.

Project 3

Study the attitudes of a group toward its leaders. Your conclusions may be strengthened in three ways: (a) More than one observer may analyze the same meeting; (b) The observer may analyze different meetings of the same group with different leaders; (c) The observer may analyze meetings of different discussion groups. (See pp. 18–20.)

Seek answers to such questions as these: How do members reflect their attitudes toward the leaders? Did members seem to react toward the leader as a person, or toward his conduct of the discussion? Does the leader's behavior seem to reflect his personality and emotional needs? Was he ill at ease? Did he seem anxious to do what the group expected of him? Could you tell how he feels about leadership from watching him in action?

Project 4

In other projects we focus attention on the duties and responsibilities of the discussion leader. But an All-American quarterback cannot reach or retain that status without the skilled and eager cooperation of the team. The analogy, we hope, is obvious. An All-American discussion requires group members who know the rules and are willing to play the game.

Observe a discussion group in action to see if this team play is evident. (See pp. 20–21.) Do members:

a. Share in developing and maintaining group values and morale?

b. Participate in planning general and specific group goals?

c. Contribute to the discussion with the apparent expectation of receiving fair and careful consideration?

d. Undertake any responsibility for sharing the leadership of the group?

e. Communicate effectively?

f. Adjust to emotional needs and tensions of others?

g. Help evaluate the group's progress toward its goals? The techniques it uses?

Project 5

At various places in this book we have stated the, to us, elementary idea that every discussion of the kinds we are writing about should have a primary purpose. The leader and members alike should be aware of that purpose and try to keep the discussion relevant. We exclude the pleasant but unpredictable and unplanned conversations that sometimes occur at the club, in the smoking car, or in the beauty parlor.

Attend one or more discussion meetings and observe the seeming presence or absence of a primary purpose. (See pp. 7–10.) The following questions should be helpful:

a. Can you phrase the purpose in a single sentence?

b. Or did the group appear to have two or more possible conflicting purposes?

c. Did group members know the purpose before they came to the meeting?

d. How does the purpose of this group affect the leader's task? Suppose, for example, that group members have definite partisan opinions based on little evidence?

e. How does the situation described above affect the preparation of members?

Project 6

The prospective leader may learn a great deal about his task by observing the work of others. In fact, he may learn as much from a poor discussion as from one that is skillfully led. Attend a discussion, paying especial attention to the following questions:

a. What was the purpose or objective of the meeting?

b. Did the group achieve or make reasonable progress toward its goal?

c. Did the group exemplify "thought in process" or group thinking?

d. Did the group reach agreement on the problem, or on any part thereof?

e. If so, was the decision based on adequate evidence?

f. Was there any evidence that those who remained silent, or nearly so, were actively thinking about the problem?

g. Was the size of the group about right for the purpose and procedure?

Project 7

Even when he really wants it, the leader finds it difficult to get an objective analysis of his work. This project has that purpose. Appoint in advance a team of four process observers. Each observer is asked to gather data on one of the following aspects of group participation. (See pp. 125–127.)

a. The number of participations made by each member, and the number who did not say anything

b. The "flow" of conversation from one member to another and from one point to the next

c. The nature of each member's contributions

d. The value of each member's contributions

Before you read the process observers' reports, evaluate your part in the meeting. List the problems that arose and what you did about them. Then examine the observers' reports to see if they agree with you and with each other.

Project 8

Have you recently observed a discussion you would classify as a failure? Or one that had serious weaknesses? To what extent were the disappointing results due to limitations in the discussion method? (See pp. 11–12.)

Consider the following questions in your analysis:

a. Was the group trying to do too much too fast?

b. Was the group attempting to discuss a problem on which members had little interest or information?

c. Was the group trying to discuss a question of fact?

d. Were some points of view ignored or inadequately presented?

e. Did members gloss over, or completely ignore, real differences of opinion in attempting to reach a consensus?

f. Were there too many comments beginning, "I think, . . ." "I feel, . . ." "Every one agrees. . . ."?

Project 9

Discussion meetings may be evaluated in various ways. We suggest here types of evidence that might be available when a group has had a number of meetings. (See pp. 118–120.)

a. How many persons attended?

b. Did everyone join in the discussion?

c. Is there any evidence of changed attitudes toward the problem?

d. Can you find any evidence of individual or group action in the problems discussed?

e. What about postmeeting conversations? Or did members immediately start for home?

f. Was there any evidence of growing interest in the problems? Were they treated in editorials? Talked about at club meetings?

Project 10

Suppose you are chairman of an evaluating committee assigned to measure as objectively as practicable the effects of a discussion or series of discussions, on participants. You have two tasks of about equal importance: (a) to analyze the expected audience, whose attitudes are sought; (b) to choose and administer the measuring device best suited to the situation. These four methods are recommended; certain others may be more accurate, but they are also more difficult to construct. (See pp. 120–123.)

a. The simple ballot
b. The shift of opinion ballot
c. The rating scale
d. The linear scale

To measure shift of opinion, prediscussion and postdiscussion tests are usually necessary. To secure frankness of response, members are usually asked *not* to sign their names. This is especially true if the topic is a "hot" issue.

Project 11

In earlier projects we have suggested the general, and largely subjective, ways of evaluating discussion meetings. Here we want to find out how much the group knows about the topic at the conclusion of the discussion, and, perhaps, how much of this information was obtained during the meeting. (See pp. 74, 120.)

Two types of tests may be used to find out how much group members know about the topic at the end of the meeting. The first type would be to ask group members to write in a series of statements either what they know about the topic or what they learned about it during the discussion. The second type of test would be a series of "True-False" statements covering as nearly as possible the information given in the meeting, as well as some additional items. The first test is easier to give but harder to score. The reverse is true of the objective test.

The simplest information test is a series of "True-False" statements. The longer the test, the more significant are the results. Since you will probably not know just what facts will be presented in the discussion, you should include facts that you think every well-informed person should know. During the meeting you can check those that are included in the discussion. This will give you scores on general informaiton and on the items given in the meeting. Directions for interpreting the signficance of the scores can be found in any college library.

A more accurate measurement of what was learned during the meeting requires pretest and posttests. Before the meeting, those present mark the Pretest form headed "What I Know About the Topic." After the discussion they mark Form B, "What I Now Know About the Topic." If panel members are given copies before the meeting, they can include most of the information included in the test.

Project 12

Suppose that instead of measuring the information gained from a discussion, you want to know its effects on the opinions or attitudes of those present. The general testing procedure is the same. The simpler tests for measuring attitudes are described on pp. 120–122. More precise tests consist of a series of statements indicating different degrees of belief about the topic. The person taking the test marks each statement:

> A. T. for Absolutely True
> P. T. for Probably True
>   ? for Don't Know
> P. F. for Probably False
> A. F. for Absolutely False

This type of test, containing opinions of varying intensity about the topic, can also be used as a basis of discussion. "Why do you believe that. . . . ?"

To learn what members believe about the topic, without regard to the source of the belief, have them mark the test at the end of the discussion. To discover the immediate effects of the discussion, members mark Form A, "What I Believe About the Topic," before the meeting, and Form B, "What I Now Believe About the Topic," after the discussion.

Project 13

Observe a fairly small discussion group in action. Do the members stand ready to assist the leader by temporarily assuming one or more of the following leadership roles? (See pp. 22–23.)

a. The morale builder
b. The conciliator
c. The compromiser
d. The expediter
e. The standard setter
f. The process observer

In some instances there is no need of role playing as far as assuming a role is concerned.

A simple check list for recording observations can be made by listing the names of the participants down the side of a sheet of paper and the leadership roles across the top. Observations on such questions as these should supplement the check list: Could you tell whether a group member was consciously playing a role? Do members feel free to shift from one role to another? Or do they stay with one role all the time? Was this good or bad? How can the results of this project be used to improve future discussions?

Project 14

This project, though similar, differs from Project 13 in two ways. In that project, the emphasis is on the discussion process and how group members may assist the leadership in following it. Here we emphasize the problem or topic and consider ways in which members can assist in its analysis and eventual solution. The projects differ, therefore, on roles which members may play during the discussion. (See p. 23.) We should note here that the word "role" does not necessarily mean "playing a part." Quite the contrary. The "inquirer" may raise pertinent questions; the "elaborator" may ask for information on an important point.

Attend a discussion and note instances where members assume the following roles:

a. The inquirer
b. The contributor
c. The elaborator
d. The reviewer
e. The evaluator
f. The energizer
g. The recorder

The form suggested for Project 13 may be used. The following questions may be helpful: Do members shift freely from one role to another? Do some members stay with one role all the time? Is this good or bad? How can this information be used to improve this or future discussions?

Project 15

If it can be arranged tactfully, attend a meeting that does not run smoothly because of the presence of a few negatively minded members. Or it may be better, unknown to the other members, to have one or two assume certain of these negative roles: (See p. 24.)

a. The dominator .   d. The security seeker
b. The blocker   e. The lobbyist
c. The cynic

How seriously did the behavior of these individuals handicap the process of discussion? The result of discussion? How did the leader attempt to deal with the "problem children"? Did group members do anything about it? With what success? What other ways of handling the situation would you have tried?

Project 16

Suppose you are chairman of a committee to arrange a public discussion meeting on a serious situation confronting your own community. Your committee has had an organization meeting and has gathered to report what has been done, and to assign each member a part in arranging and conducting the meeting.

At the first meeting, the committee considered the community's information about the problem, and the general inclination to resist change. The group also decided the purpose and goal of the discussion and phrased the question for discussion.

These items are on the agenda for this meeting. Note that the answer to one question sometimes influences the answer to the next.

a. Estimating the attendance.

b. Choosing the time and place for the meeting.

c. Deciding the type of discussion best suited for meetings of the estimated size.

d. Choosing the leader or moderator and the public discussion speakers.

e. Preparing to publicize the meeting.

f. Appointing a discussion team (if desired).

g. Preparing a program to be distributed to the audience members. This should include a time schedule for the speakers and rules governing audience participation in the forum.

Project 17

You are asked to have charge of "Discussion 66" for a large public discussion meeting. Because this device for giving everyone in the audience the chance to participate in the forum period must be explained and conducted in a very short time, the instructions and forms used for reporting group reaction must be prepared and pretested in advance.

We list here in chronological order the steps you should take in this assignment:

a. Be sure you understand the point on which audience response is desired. Discussion 66 has been used to choose from a list of projects the group wishes to investigate, to frame a question the group would like to have answered by "top brass," and to get a "Yes-No" answer on a policy question.

b. Prepare and pretest a short statement explaining the nature and importance of the assignment. This statement should be mimeographed and handed to audience members as they arrive for the meeting. It should include directions for dividing the audience into groups of six and the method of choosing chairmen and secretaries.

c. Prepare and pretest the question or list of alternatives on which group response is desired. This should also be included in the mimeographed statement.

d. Prepare, on 4 by 6 cards, directions for the chairman of the groups of six.

e. Prepare, on 5 by 7 cards, forms to be used by the secretaries of the groups in reporting group decisions. It would be helpful if cards of different color are used for chairmen and secretaries.

f. Have a committee of helpers ready to distribute the cards as soon as the group chairmen and secretaries are chosen. Announce whether the secretaries are to report orally or to hand in the cards.

g. In your introductory statement at the meeting announce

the time limits (sometimes eight or ten minutes rather than six) and see that they are observed. Explain why the information is important and how it will be used.

Project 18

Suppose you are asked to have charge of role playing for a discussion meeting. Since there are two widely different kinds of role playing, the first step is to decide which is best adapted to the problem, the purpose, and the personnel of the group.

The first type is prepared and rehearsed in advance. It consists of one or more dramatizations—from two to four minutes in length—written to portray one phase or issue of the problem before the group. The parts are spoken by "actors." The audience knows the actors are playing roles, rather than voicing their own opinions. These scenes are sometimes recorded and used by various groups. These dramatizations are used to start the discussion or to focus attention on "hot issues," on which group members might remain silent. When well done, this type of role playing may present a situation more vividly than may come from spontaneous discussion. It may be used before fairly large audiences.

Extemporaneous role playing has been publicized by writers on group dynamics. They advocate its use in conferences and workshops, especially those dealing with various kinds of group and community problems. Membership in these groups is restricted in size to not more than 40 or 50; and to those having a professional interest in the problems under investigation. In these situations, role playing is used whenever the leader thinks it would be helpful in getting the other fellow's point of view. The leader appoints members to represent the different persons or groups involved in the situation. The "cast" leaves the room for a few minutes to make a brief outline of the plot. They return and put on the scene, extemporizing their lines. Until members become accustomed to this method, the leader should be careful to appoint only those who have confidence in their ability to take the assigned role. Those who suffer from stage fright may leave the room and keep on going!

Your assignment for the first type of role playing resembles that of the play director. You get someone to write the scripts, select the cast, and supervise the rehearsal. For extempore role playing preparation is more difficult. The best you can do is to select a half dozen members who like the challenge of extemporizing lines, and have them practice on simple plots. Sometimes this type of role playing is very, very good but when it is bad it is horrid.

Project 19

Analyze a discussion group with which you are familiar. Record the presence or absence of the following types of group behavior. From your notes construct a "personality profile." (See pp. 15–17.)

a. Group conformity
b. Group prejudice
c. Group resistance to change
d. Group structure
e. Group values
f. Group patterns of discussion
g. Group patterns of decision.

The amateur analyst will probably not be able to look for all these factors at once. If it is more than a learning device for the leader, the project should be assigned to a committee.

Project 20

This project represents an attempt to apply the "group personality" project to a specific situation. (See pp. 15–17.) Attend a discussion and try to find answers to such questions as these:

a. Do group members seem accustomed to express their views freely?

b. How are prejudices avoided, overcome, or utilized?

c. What techniques would you suggest to help the group lessen its resistance to change?

d. What subgroups exist? Can they be made helpful rather than destructive to the group project?

e. How can prevalent group values be linked to the discussion of a specific topic?

f. How can the accepted patterns of decision be utilized in solving a specific problem?

Project 21

The film "How to Conduct a Discussion" states and comments on these eleven pieces of advice or principles of discussion:

a. The physical setting should be attractive and comfortable.

b. There should be a good social feeling among group members.

c. The leader should have a basic plan but be flexible in the use of it.

d. There should be direct interchange of information and opinions among members.

e. The path of progress should be kept open for each individual member.

f. The experience of group members should be used to enrich the discussion.

g. All members should feel a responsibility for the effective conduct of the group.

h. All members should understand both immediate and ultimate goals.

i. Methods and procedures should be as varied as possible.

j. The group should base its discussion on fact and experience as well as on opinion.

k. All members should try to improve the group performance.

If this film is available it might well be used for a "Film Forum." Each member of the group should report on two or three of the above "principles." If the film is not available, the points may be discussed in other types of discussion meetings.

Appendix B

Reference and Resource Materials for Discussion Leaders

DISCUSSION LEADERS AND THOSE WHO TEACH discussion courses sometimes want additional materials on discussion techniques and sources of information on specific topics for discussion. The suggestions that follow represent selected materials and sources available when this book was written.

I. Reference Materials on Discussion Techniques

A. GENERAL REFERENCES

The following publications may be particularly helpful as supplementary and background reading for those who teach courses in discussion.

1. *Adult Leadership,* a monthly publication of the Adult Education Association, 743 N. Wabash Ave., Chicago 11, Illinios.
2. Chase, Stuart, *Power of Words,* New York, Harcourt, Brace and Co., 1954.
3. Chase, Stuart, *Roads to Agreement,* New York, Harper & Brothers, 1951.
4. Ewbank, Henry Lee, and Auer, J. Jeffery, *Discussion and Debate,* New York, Appleton-Century-Crofts, Inc., 1951.
5. Fansler, Thomas, *Creative Power Through Discussion,* New York, Harper & Brothers, 1950.

6. Flesch, Rudolf, *The Art of Clear Thinking,* New York, Harper & Brothers, 1951.
7. Lasker, Bruno, *Democracy Through Discussion,* New York, H. W. Wilson Co., 1950.
8. Lee, Irving J., *Customs and Crises In Communication,* New York, Harper & Brothers, 1954.
9. Lee, Irving J., *How to Talk with People,* New York, Harper & Brothers, 1952.
10. Strauss, Bert, and Strauss, Frances, *New Ways to Better Meetings,* New York, Viking Press, 1951.
11. Thelen, Herbert A., *Dynamics of Groups at Work,* Chicago, University of Chicago Press, 1954.
12. Whyte, William F., "Leadership and Group Participation," *Bulletin,* Ithaca, N. Y., New York State School of Industrial and Labor Relations, Cornell University, May, 1953.

B. DISCUSSION FOR YOUTH GROUPS

These publications, especially adapted to the problems of "teen-age" discussion groups, will be helpful for teachers and leaders.

1. Junior Town Meeting League, 400 S. Front St., Columbus 15, Ohio, publishes the pamphlets: *Make Youth Discussion Conscious!* (1948), *Teaching Controversial Issues* (1948), *Learning Through Group Discussion* (1949), *Using Current Materials* (1950), *Developing Discussion in School and Community* (1951), *Youth Discussion: Formats and Techniques* (1953).
2. National Association of Secondary-School Principals, "Public Address in the Secondary School," *Bulletin,* Washington, D.C., May, 1952.
3. Stiles, Lindley J., and Dorsey, Mattie F., *Democratic Teaching in Secondary Schools,* Philadelphia, J. B. Lippincott Company, 1950.

C. DISCUSSION IN INDUSTRY

Those who are concerned with discussion methods in industrial, or labor-management, communication will find these publications of special interest.

1. Blum, Fred H., *Toward a Democratic Work Process,* New York, Harper & Brothers, 1953.
2. Busch, Henry M., *Conference Methods in Industry,* New York, Harper & Brothers, 1949.
3. Perry, John, *Human Relations in Small Industry,* (Catalog No. SDP 1.12:3), Washington, D. C., U. S. Government Printing Office, 1953.
4. Raines, I. I., *Better Communications in Small Business,* (Catalog No. SBA 1.12:7), Washington, D. C., U. S. Government Printing Office, 1953.

D. Parliamentary Procedure

For leaders of discussion groups which become "action groups," and for business meetings of all organizations, these publications will be useful. The first is a brief handbook, the second a textbook, the third a standard guide.

1. Auer, J. Jeffery, *Essentials of Parliamentary Procedure,* New York, Appleton-Century-Crofts, Inc., 1942.
2. O'Brien, Joseph F., *Parliamentary Law for the Layman,* New York, Harper & Brothers, 1953.
3. Robert, Henry M., *Robert's Rules of Order, Revised,* Chicago, Scott, Foresman and Co., 1951.

E. Reports of Experimental Research

For those interested in research studies on discussion, leadership, and the group process, these compilations should be helpful.

1. Cartwright, Dorwin, and Zander, Alvin, eds., *Group Dynamics: Research and Theory,* Evanston, Ill., Row, Peterson and Co., 1953.
2. Sherif, Muzafer, and Wilson, M. O., eds., *Group Relations at the Crossroads,* New York, Harper & Brothers, 1953.
3. Strodtbeck, Fred L., and Hare, A. Paul, "Bibliography of Small Group Research," *Sociometry,* May, 1954.

F. Transcripts of Discussions

One good way of learning about leading discussion is listening to discussions; another is reading printed transcripts of discussions. Here are some:

1. *American Forum of the Air,* Ransdell, Inc., Washington 18, D.C.
2. Garland, Jasper V., ed., *Discussion Methods: Explained and Illustrated,* New York, H. W. Wilson Co., 1951.
3. *Northwestern Reviewing Stand,* Director of Radio, Northwestern University, Evanston, Illinois.
4. *Town Meeting,* America's Town Meeting of the Air, New York, Columbia University Press.
5. *University of Chicago Round Table,* Chicago, University of Chicago Press.

G. FILMS

The films listed below are designed for leaders and members of discussion groups, and are suitable for both teen-agers and adults. They are in black-and-white, with sound, and run from 10 to 25 minutes. When used by leaders or teachers they should be followed by a discussion period in which listeners can evaluate and think about how to apply what they have learned. These films may be purchased from the producers, or rented from the film library of the extension divisions of most state universities or from commercial firms.

1. Bureau of Publications, Teachers College, Columbia University, New York, *Meeting in Session.*
2. Coronet Films, Inc., Coronet Building, Chicago 1, Ill., *Discussion in Democracy, Learning from Discussion, Parliamentary Procedure.*
3. Encyclopaedia Britannica Films, Inc., Wilmette, Ill., *Room for Discussion, Organizing Discussion Groups, How to Conduct a Discussion.*
4. Young America Films, Inc., 18 E. 41st St., New York 19, *Speech: Conducting a Meeting.*

II. Resource Materials on Topics for Discussion

Facts and opinions about topics to be discussed need not all come from the printed page; leaders should encourage participants to prepare themselves by discussing the topic in advance with nonmembers, by making surveys of opinions, and by doing a little plain "settin' and thinkin.'" Then, before doing more of the latter, they should examine published materials relating to the topic. Here are suggestions, some of them obvious, about locating resource materials.

A. LIBRARIES

Most librarians are equipped to suggest specific books, pamphlets, or articles. They may have prepared bibliographies on the topic for discussion. In addition to the library's books, its periodicals may be fruitful, especially the *Atlantic Monthly, Foreign Affairs Quarterly, Fortune, Harper's, Nation, New Republic, Newsweek, Progressive, Time, U. S. News and World Report,* and *Vital Speeches.*

B. UNIVERSITY EXTENSION DIVISIONS

The extension divisions of most state universities maintain special services for discussion and debate groups, such as bibliographies, packets of selected materials, lending libraries, and even resource personnel on special topics and on discussion procedures.

C. ORGANIZATIONS

Numerous organizations have been established to promote special causes or points of view on current issues, and are happy to send pertinent literature to those interested. Among such organizations, for example, are the C.I.O., the League of Women Voters, the National Association of Manufacturers, and the United Nations Association. A complete list of nearly 900 such organizations, with addresses, can be found in the *World Almanac.*

D. SERIAL PUBLICATIONS ON CURRENT ISSUES

In addition to the resources already listed, discussion leaders should be aware of certain publications which appear at regular intervals, deal with current public issues, and are especially adaptable as background and reference materials for discussions of these issues. Here is a selected list.

1. *American Education Press,* 400 S. Front St., Columbus 15, Ohio. Publishes "Our Times," weekly survey of current affairs containing a guide for a Junior Town Meeting League discussion topic.

2. *Armed Forces Talk,* Office of the Secretary of Defense, Superintendent of Documents, Government Printing Office, Washington 25, D.C. Weekly discussion guide on current national and international topics.

3. *Congressional Digest,* 1631 K St., N.W., Washington 6, D.C. Monthly pro-and-con treatment of a current public problem.

4. Discussion guides: *American Mercury, Newsweek, Reader's Digest,* and *Time* are among the popular magazines maintaining a discussion service, including background materials and discussion guides. The Parent-Teacher Association magazine includes discussion materials and guides in each issue.

5. *Foreign Policy Reports* and *Headline Books,* Foreign Policy Association, 22 E. 38th St., New York 18, N.Y. Regular publications dealing with American foreign policy and international relations.

6. *Public Affairs Pamphlets,* Public Affairs Committee, 50 Rockefeller Plaza, New York 20, N.Y. Regular series of pamphlets on national and world affairs, with bibliographies for further reading.

7. *Reference Shelf,* H. W. Wilson Co., 950–972 University Ave., New York 52, N.Y. Annual series of handbooks, each dealing with a special problem in public affairs, and presenting all points of view through excerpts from other publications, speeches, etc.

Index